Henry Anstice

Annals of St. Luke's church, Rochester, N.Y. 1817-1883

Henry Anstice

Annals of St. Luke's church, Rochester, N.Y. 1817-1883

ISBN/EAN: 9783337261191

Printed in Europe, USA, Canada, Australia, Japan

Cover: Foto ©Lupo / pixelio.de

More available books at **www.hansebooks.com**

ST. LUKE'S CHURCH. ERECTED 1824.

" Here holy thoughts a light have shed
    From many a radiant face,
And prayers of humble virtue made
    The perfume of the place.
And anxious hearts have pondered here
    The mystery of life,
And prayed the eternal Light to clear
    Their doubts, and aid their strife."

ANNALS

OF

ST. LUKE'S CHURCH,

ROCHESTER, N. Y.

1817–1883

WITH

NAMES OF OFFICERS, PAROCHIAL STATISTICS

AND

HISTORICAL SKETCHES

OF THE

OTHER PARISHES.

BY THE

REV. HENRY ANSTICE, D. D.

"Hæc olim meminisse juvabit."

ROCHESTER:

SCRANTOM, WETMORE & CO.

1883

PREFATORY NOTE.

THE ANNALS OF ST. LUKE'S CHURCH are published in compliance with the request of St. Luke's Vestry as contained in the following preamble and resolution adopted by that body in July last :

" WHEREAS St. Luke's Parish has now had an organized existence extending over two generations, and the facts of its history are of interest sufficient to warrant their preservation in permanent and accessible form, therefore

RESOLVED, that our Rector be requested to prepare and publish in suitable book form, an Historical Sketch of St. Luke's Church, embodying such documentary and statistical facts as he shall deem of interest."

Sketches of the other parishes are appended as no history of the mother-church would be complete without some record of the origin and growth of those organizations which, proceeding from her more or less directly, are her fellow workers in the field of Rochester.

No effort has been spared to secure absolute accuracy in facts and figures, and in every case original sources of information have been consulted where accessible.

The epistolary extracts in the earlier part of the Sketch
were taken from the " Hobart Correspondence," which
is in the archives of the General Convention.

The kind co-operation of the clergymen and laymen
who have afforded facilities for the researches necessary
in the preparation of this work, or whose personal
reminiscences have been of value, is hereby gratefully
acknowledged.

It has been throughout the simple design of the author
to give a clear, accurate and concise embodiment of
facts and figures without aiming at grace of expression
or indulging in personal characterizations of men or
measures.

In memory of those that have gone before, who have
been "careful to maintain good works," and to the
zealous workers of to-day, these Annals are inscribed.

ST. LUKE'S RECTORY. Sept. 1, 1883.

Contents.

Historical Sketch.

The organization of St. Luke's Parish was effected by the Rev. Henry U. Onderdonk, "Rector of St. John's Church, Canandaigua, and Missionary in parts adjacent," on the 14th day of July, 1817, under the corporate name of 'St. Luke's Church, Genesee Falls."

The original corporators, as indicated by their signatures to the "Declaration of Attachment to the Protestant Episcopal Church," were S. Melancton Smith, Moses P. Belknap, Wm. Y. Green, Jesse Moore, A. G. Dauby, John P. Comparet, Anson House, Daniel Hibbard, Jacob Howe, Elisha Johnson, Jonah Brown, Caleb Hammond, Jabez Wilkinson, Joseph Thompson, Wm. Atkinson, Sam'l J. Andrews, John C. Rochester, John Mastick, Silas Smith, Roswell Babbit, Enos Stone, Oliver Culver, John P. Sheldon, Daniel Tinker, Lewis Jenkins, H. Montgomery, Joseph Spencer, Joseph Griffin. This instrument bore date March 13, 1817, at

which time the Rev. Mr. Onderdonk "held the
first public services of our Church at Rochesterville."

The requisite legal notice having been "read
at morning service on the two Sundays next
preceding" the date of organization, twenty of
the above-named persons met in a schoolhouse,
belonging to Samuel James Andrews, on the
east side of the river, in what was known as the
town of Brighton, in the county of Ontario.
The Rev. Mr. Onderdonk presided and the
Rev. Geo. H. Norton offered prayer.   Roswell
Babbitt acted as clerk.   Col. N. Rochester and
Samuel J. Andrews were elected Wardens, and
Silas Smith, Roswell Babbit, John Mastick,
Lewis Jenkins, Elisha Johnson, John C. Rochester, Wm. Atkinson and Oliver Culver, Vestrymen.   The original Certificate of Incorpora-
tion was recorded in the Clerk's office of Ontario
County, on the 19th of July, 1817, in Liber C
of Miscellaneous Records, at page 195.

The first stated services were held by the
Rev. George H. Norton, whose entrance upon
the field is chronicled in the following extracts
from letters addressed to Bishop Hobart by the
Rev. Mr. Onderdonk.   Under date of Canandaigua, Jan. 14, 1817, he writes—

"Mr. Norton passed his first two examina-
tions a week ago very creditably.   In the hope

that he will remain in the West, and believing
that he is qualified to be very useful, I shall
venture to begin operations at Rochesterville
pretty soon. But if he is decidedly spoken
of there as the missionary for building them
up, it will be highly proper that he go there the
instant he is in Orders."

And again under date of June 11, 1817,

"Mr. Norton, I hope, will go to Rochesterville, but I confess that Buffalo is more promising and more in need of him; and if Mr.
Norton goes to Buffalo, I should like to secure
Mr. Asahel Davis, or somebody, without delay
at R. Indeed Rochesterville has disappointed
me not a little. When requested to go there,
I told a gentleman I could do but little person-
ally; but they will do almost nothing themselves. But while I am there, they soon get in
order again and zealous, but so speedily relax
that they have not given the legal notices previous to organizing. Still the materials are
good, and they only want a clergyman fixed
there to get on very well. . . . . They
had $1300 subscribed at R. for a church, but
owing to the pressure of the times and I sus-
pect to difficulty in regard to a site and I fear
to unsoundness in an individual or two, the subscription went no further. Still I regard the
place as more promising than any except Buf-

falo, and more promising than that for the
mere building of a church, as materials are very
cheap at Rochesterville."

The actual organization of the parish is thus
reported by the missionary to Bishop Hobart,
under date July 15, 1817.

"Mr. Norton having supplied my place for
the last two Sundays, I devoted the morning
of each of them to Rochesterville. The proper
notices had been given and we yesterday met to
organize. The number of names had been increased from 12 to 28 attached to the Episcopal
Church; of these 20 attended the meeting and
a highly respectable Vestry was chosen. The
name is 'St. Luke's Church, Genesee Falls.'
Everything I see and learn adds to the conviction that we did not begin there too early, —the
village continues to increase. In the afternoon
of both Sundays I attended at Carthage, a new
village two miles lower down the river, and held
a third service at Pittsford, ten or eleven miles
this side of Carthage. Whether congregations
can be formed at these places is doubtful, but
we shall probably gather some gleanings at
least. Mr. Norton has charge of the three
places. He requested me to urge your sending
a clergyman to Buffalo and to Batavia if possible, as a Presbyterian clergyman has just gone

there; he will devote some of his time to them and Leroy."

In September, 1818, Bishop Hobart made his first Episcopal visitation to the infant parish and confirmed four persons—Samuel G. Andrews, Mariette Andrews, (Mrs. W. P. Shearman), Mrs. Mary E. Montgomery, and Hannah Ann Andrews, (Mrs. Swan), in the building occupied by the 1st Presbyterian society on Carroll, now State St., which was kindly placed at his disposal for the service.

From this time the occasional ministrations of the Rev. Mr. Norton were withdrawn, and for the ensuing eighteen months, some five or six services by the Rev. H. U. Onderdonk and the Rev. Alanson W. Welton, Missionary in Ontario county, were all that were held in the parish; the place of service being the school-house on the lot adjoining the present church edifice.

In the Spring of 1820, the slumbering interest in the Church was roused to the necessity of securing more frequent ministrations, and an arrangement was effected with the Rev. A. W. Welton "to perform Divine Service once in three weeks for one year;" but the removal of Mr. Welton to Detroit in a few months, terminated this engagement.

The new Vestry, however, elected at the

Easter meeting, the first convened since the
organization, consisting of George G. Sill and
William Atkinson, Wardens, and Roswell Bab-
bit, A. G. Dauby, J. Stebbins, Silas Smith, J.
Mastick, S. M. Smith, J. H. Gregory and E.
Johnson, determined to establish the parish on
a permanent basis. The offer of the original
proprietors of "the 100-acre tract," Messrs.
Rochester, Fitzhugh & Carroll, "to convey lot
No. 85 to the first religious society that should
take possession of the same and build a church
thereon," being still open, the Vestry resolved,
July 10, 1820, to avail itself of the proposition.
Before the lot, however, was definitely secured,
an effort was made in the Roman Catholic
interest to forestall the Vestry, and a messenger was sent to Geneseo to secure the signatures
of Messrs. Fitzhugh and Carroll, who resided in
that locality, to a deed of gift. But the Vestry
despatched Mr. Henry E. Rochester, then a
lad of fourteen years, on a fleeter horse with a
similar object in view. The latter succeeded
in overtaking and passing the other messenger,
who was tarrying for refreshment in the tavern
at Avon, and so obtained the necessary signatures, to which that of the senior proprietor
was cheerfully added. Meanwhile, the Vestry
had taken practical possession by digging for a
foundation and drawing building material upon
the lot.

A site being thus secured, the construction of a wooden building, 38 x 46 feet, to contain about forty pews, was decided upon, and a contract entered into, Aug. 5, 1820, with Elias Beach and Phelps Smith, to build the same, at a cost of $1260, and $200 additional for a bell tower —the building committee consisting of Col. N. Rochester, John Mastick, Harvey Montgomery and George G. Sill. The funds were provided by the following unique subscription, which is given with the spelling and capitalization as in the original:

" We the subscribers for value received, promise to pay to the Church-Wardens and Vestrymen of St. Luke's Church, in the Village of Rochesterville, and their successors in office, the several sums set opposite our respective names, on demand ; for the purpose and in trust to build a church in said Rochesterville for said St. Luke's Church : and upon the further trust that the said Church-Wardens and Vestrymen, and their successors in office, shall, after the completion of said church, sell or dispose of the pews or slips therein, and out of the funds arising therefrom, shall refund to the subscribers, with interest, the several sums by them subscribed and paid, if such funds shall be adequate : if inadequate, then to each subscriber ratably, till the funds so arising, are exhausted.

Dated, July 3, 1820.

Names.		Am't.
N. Rochester,	in lumber	$200
H. Montgomery,	in Cash	100
James Fraser,	in shelf goods	25
Wm. P. Shearman,	in goods	25

2

Names.		Am t.
Oliver Culver	(by request S. M. S.) Cash	20
S. Melancton Smith,	in Goods	25
Jonathan Child	(by H. M.) in Lumber	50
Elisha Ely	(by request S. M. S.) in Lumber	50
Frederick F. Backus.	Cash	25
William Cobb.	in Blacksmithing	25
Elisha Taylor.	in Tailoring work	10
Jas. H. Gregory,	Cash	25
West & Clark,	in Labor, Painting	25
Roswell Babbit.	in Cash	25
A. Hamlin.	in Goods	10
Silas Smith (by request S. M. S) in Goods		25
J N. Stebbins.	in goods	25
Wm. Haywood.	in Hats	20
Weston & Everest.	in Shoemaking	20
Abraham Plumb,	Goods	20
Ira West & Co.,	in Goods	10
W. W. Mumford,	in Cash	20
Ebenezer Watts, Jun'r.	tinware	10
Elwood & Colman,	in Labour	30
Wm Brewster.	in Cabinet furniture	10
William Atkinson,	in flour	25
Samuel J. Andrews.	4,000 ft. Lumber (a $8	32
Enos Stone,	one thousand feet Lumber	8
Bissell and Ely.	in lumber, 6¼M. ft.	50
E. Peck & Co..	in Books or Stationery	20
Jno. G. Vought.	in Labor	25
S. Cleveland	in Sundries	25
John Harford.	Goods	10
John Swift.	in work	25
George Cameron.	in Tailoring	8
Russell Ensworth	(will do something, S. M. S.)	
T. Bingham.	in work	8
R. King.	in work	10
H. Scrantom,	in flour or goods	7
S. H. Packard.	in chairs	8
Jehial Barnard,	in tailoring	5
Benj. James.	in coopering	5
Frederick Hanford.	in Shingles	20
Henry Draper.	in team work	25
Abner Wakelee.	in shoes	10
E. Pomeroy.	Cash	5
Zimri Davis.	in teem work	5
John G. Bond.	in lumber or team work	6

Names.		Am't.
Jacob Gould,	in goods	10
J. Mastick,	eighteen dollars cash	18
Elias Beach,	in joiner work	30
Phelps Smith,	in joiner work	30
John Bingham,	in joiner work	10

The following additional subscription, bearing date August 1, 1820, provided for the erection of a Steeple or Cupola:

Abrm. Plumb,	donation in goods	$20
West & Clark,	in Labor, painting	25
John Mastick,	in goods out of J. Spencer's Store	5
S. Melancton Smith,	in Goods	5
Silas Smith,	in Goods or demand in notes	5
J. N. Stebbins,	in goods	5
A. Reynolds,	in goods or brick	5
D. D. Barnard,	in Cider and apples del'd at Mendon	5
Preston Smith,	in Goods at his Grocery	5
E. Watts	will do the sodering for the Cupulo.	
Levi Ward, jr.,	goods or provisions	5
Elisha Ely,	in Lumber	25
Elisha Taylor,	in Tayloring work	10
Daniel Warren, in mason work when called for with one week's Notice		10
Robert King,	in Joiner work	5
Jonathan Case, in mason work, with one week's notice		10
Martin Clapp,	in mason work at six days notice	10
Robert W. Churchill,	in joiner work	10
Asa Bartlett,	Mason work	5
John Meeker,	in joiner work on or before thirty days	10
A. Steward		5
N. T. Rochester,	in Lumber	5
Timothy Bosworth, to be paid in Combs at cash prices		5
W. L. Whiting, in goods at J. Spencer's Store for improvements on church		10
Joshua Ross,	five dollars in Meat	5
Richmon Tuttle,	Ten Dollars in Saddlery for improvement on the church	10

16   ANNALS OF ST. LUKE'S.

Names.		Am't.
Ephm. Moore, five Dollars in Pork out of my Shop for improvement on church		
Moses Dyer,	two dollars in meat when called for	2
David Stone,	five Dollars in Joiner's work with one week's notice	5
Ashbel Steele,	10 Dollars in mason work	10
Samuel Graves,	$5 In Blacksmith work	5
William Atkinson,	in flour	5
Silas Smith,	one dollar Cash	pd
S. Melancton Smith,	one dollar Cash	paid
William Atkinson,	one dollar Cash	paid
James H. Gregory,	one dollar Cash	pd
J. N. Stebbins,	one dollar Cash	pd
R. Babbit,	one dollar Cash	pd
N. Rochester pd building chimney	$4.06	
Brick, rent of Stove, etc.	6.35 pd	
		10.41
Smith & Alcott		9.18

Pending the erection of the church, the following letter was addressed to Bishop Hobart by William Atkinson, Warden, in behalf of the Wardens and Vestrymen, under date Rochester, Nov. 10, 1820, (the title of the village corporation having been changed in 1819 by an act of the legislature from Rochesterville to Rochester), which sets forth fully the condition of the parish at this time:

"We presume, ere this, you have been informed by our friend Mr. Onderdonk, of the progress of our small society in erecting a house of public worship in this place, which, by the blessing of Providence, we intend to finish by the latter end of December. We have long been desirous of procuring a young clergyman,

who would command respect by his talents and
esteem by his virtues, and who would be in
every way calculated to raise a society from a
small beginning to a respectable size. It appears to us that here is a field for a clergyman
to become eminently useful by an acquisition
of members to the Church. We feel gratified
on hearing that a person of this description has
been found in Mr. Cuming, who, in your opinion, is every way calculated and who seems disposed to come. One great difficulty, however,
arises in procuring ample funds for his support,
owing to the smallness of our society and want
of means. We, therefore, make application for
some assistance from your missionary fund, or
in any way deemed proper by yourself. We
can probably raise three hundred dollars by
great exertion and great liberality by our members, all of whom will contribute to the best of
their ability; and by an addition of two hundred and fifty dollars from your fund, we shall
be able to establish such a respectable standing
as to make up any deficiency by those who would
soon be added to our numbers. As our population increases with an unexampled rapidity
and many persons of wealth, talent and respectability are daily added to our society, it be-
comes highly important for the Church that in
the commencement there be established among

us a man of respectable talents ; and that some
assistance be granted for his support from
abroad, so that an insupportable tax be not laid
on a few individual members in the beginning,
and consequently prevent an acquisition of
members. A very few years will place us in a
situation so as not to require foreign aid. We
would thank you to take our situation under
your serious consideration, feeling confident
that every exertion will be made by you for
our assistance, and would be pleased to hear
from you previous to our communicating with
Mr. Cuming on the subject. Be so good, also,
as to inform us whether there would be an im-
propriety in performing Divine Service in the
church before consecration. Mr. Onderdonk
has, no doubt, shown you a communication
from Col. Rochester, expressive of the minds
of the Vestry."

The application for aid in the foregoing letter was fortified by the following communication to the Bishop from the Rev. Mr. Cuming,
who was already at this date, Dec. 4, 1820, upon
the ground, having come from Binghampton,
where he held a missionary appointment :

" Yesterday, for the first time, I officiated in
this place. The attention was both general
and flattering. The prospect is good. In the

evening I went to Penfield. Something may be done there bye-and-bye.

" The Church will be ready for consecration the 1st of January. Will you have the goodness to inform me as early as possible on what day you will consecrate it, and of the other places in this vicinity you will expect to visit, and whether you will officiate at them morning or afternoon. I expect to take Priests' Orders when you are here,—will you preach or shall some one of the clergy in this part of the country do it.

"As my living in this place will not exceed four hundred dollars per annum, I trust I shall be continued on the missionary list."

The young parish, however, was apparently thought able to take care of itself, as no assistance was received. The Vestry accordingly entered into agreement Jan. 10, 1821, with the Rev. F. H. Cuming, Deacon, " to perform divine service in such manner as is customary in well regulated Protestant Episcopal Churches in the State of New York, for the term of one year from and after the first Sunday in December, 1820;" for which service the Vestry agreed to pay the sum of four hundred and seventy-five dollars; which sum was increased at various times, until in December, 1823, the salary was fixed at eight hundred dollars.

The little church was first occupied on Christmas Day and was consecrated by Bishop Hobart on the 20th of February ensuing, at which time also the Rite of Confirmation was administered to the following persons: John Mastick, Jared N. Stebbins, Elbert Scrantom, N. T. Rochester, Ann Cornelia Rochester, Dorothy Stebbins, Frances Tiffany and Sarah Mason.

On the following day, the Rev. Mr. Cuming was advanced to the Priesthood.

In his convention address of that year, the Bishop in mentioning these facts, adds : " It gives me great pleasure to see a respectable and increasing congregation in a flourishing village, the site of which at the Falls of the Genesee river a few years since was a wilderness."

The prosperity of the parish under the ministry of Mr. Cuming, rendered increased accommodation necessary, and accordingly on the 25th of June, 1823, the Vestry resolved to build a new church when the subscription should amount to eight thousand dollars. It was hoped that Trinity Church, New York, would loan two thousand dollars more, and the Rev. Mr. Cuming was authorized and requested Aug. 12, to draft a petition to this effect to that corporation. The application, however, proved unsuccessful. The following letter from Mr.

Cuming to Bishop Hobart under date Aug. 15. 1823, explains the situation :

" It is now about two and a half years since the Church in this place had the constant services of a clergyman. Five communicants were all that could at the commencement of this period be found residing here. The number of individuals in the place who had been educated Episcopalians amounted to twenty. Though we are still but a little flock, our increase has been greater than the most sanguine of us expected to see within so short a period. At the very beginning every effort was made to prevent our permanent establishment. These efforts have continued to be made, but at no time with more determination than at present. It is unnecessary for me to go into details. I have an account of facts treasured up with respect to the hostility displayed toward the Church here, the disclosure of which would even make almost every opposer of our institutions in every other place to which my knowledge extends, blush. The most unremitting exertions are made, and the most ungentlemanly acts resorted to to keep people, especially those of influence, enterprise and capital away from the Church and induce them to attend elsewhere. . . . . . It is highly important to the welfare of the Church, and especially to her

increase in respectability and wealth, that we
erect a building which shall reflect credit upon
the architect, upon the village and the Church
at large."

The infant parish thus obliged to be depend-
ent on its own resources, determined to "arise
and build." In September, 1823, the Vestry
resolved to enter into a contract with H. T.
McGeorge to build a stone church 53 x 73 with
a tower 16 x 6 at the contract price of $9,000,
and William Pitkin, Caleb L. Clark, S. M.
Smith, T. H. Rochester and Silas Smith with
the minister *ex officio*, were appointed the building committee. The cost of the edifice, however, reached the sum of $10,400. The old
frame church was removed to the rear of the
lot and was subsequently used for Sunday
School purposes until 1832, when the building
was sold, removed to Buffalo St., converted to
secular uses and finally demolished in April,
1875.

The corner stone of the new structure was
laid May 11, 1824, and the edifice was first
opened for public worship Sept. 4, 1825.
The following contemporary description is taken
from the first Rochester Directory, published in
1827 :

"The style of the building, is Gothick, which
has been rigidly observed in every particular.

The main part of the front is of hewn gray
stone from Auburn. The two corners of the
tower and the two corners of the body of the
house are of red freestone, as are also the water
table, the caps, sills and jambs of the windows
and doors. The two windows in the tower are
strikingly beautiful, containing a proper number of spandrels and branching mullions, and
ornamented with rich and delicate tracery.
Around the arch of the first of these, handsomely cut in the stone cap, is the name of the
church, with the year of its erection. The
tower is 16 feet square, projecting five feet be-
yond the body of the church, and rising to the
height of 90 feet. This is finished at the top
with eight pinnacles, connected by a castellated
or embattled balustrade. A similar balustrade
runs around the roof of the whole house,
having similar pinnacles at each corner. The
wood-work on the outside of the house has
been made strongly to resemble the red freestone, by a process termed *smalting*.

" In the arrangement of the interiour will be
seen convenience, elegance, and a strict econ-
omy of room. The pulpit and desk consist of
a number of delicate Gothick arches, behind
which is a drapery of dark blue velvet. The
chancel is in the form of an oval, placed in
front of the desk, and containing a Communion

Table of Italian marble, and a baptismal font of the purest alabaster, resting on a pedestal of agate marble. The gallery is supported by large cluster columns, painted in imitation of light blue variegated marble. The ceiling is finished with intersecting vaulted or groined arches, ornamented with stucco work. In the church is placed a large and remarkably fine-toned organ."

This organ was built by Hall & Erben of New York and cost $1300; the instrumental music in the old church having been furnished by a violin, flute, clarionet and bass viol. The first organist was Daniel Clark, who held the position till May, 1827, when he was superseded by William Staunton, remaining however in charge of the choir until April, 1828. The engagement authorized to be made with the new organist was " at a salary of $200 per annum and a guarantee of ten scholars in music @ $10 per year for one year."

The pews were "offered at public sale on perpetual lease, and for one or three years by bids for choice at the valuation and annual rents affixed in the schedule attached." The highest valuation was $280, and the highest annuity $20. The number of pews on the ground floor was sixty-six, and in the gallery twenty-six.

The church was consecrated by Bishop Hobart, Sept. 30, 1826, the ceremony having been thus long delayed owing to the Bishop's absence in Europe.

The christian activity of the parish found expression, March 2, 1827, in the organization of the " Female Benevolent and Auxiliary Missionary Society," whose object was " the procuring of funds in aid of plans and societies formed for the purpose of promoting the cause of religion as connected with the interests of the Prot. Epis. Church, special reference being had to the wants of the General Missionary Society of the Episcopal Church and the Monroe County Episcopal Association, for disseminating religious knowledge." This last-named association, organized in February, 1827, appears to have allowed the object for which it was formed, viz., " the supply of vacant places within the county with the services of the Episcopal Church, assisting in the establishment and support of new congregations, and the formation of Sunday Schools," to devolve entirely upon the ladies' society, designed to be auxiliary to it. This organization, however, devoted itself at once to earnest work, with a membership of 126, and with Mrs. Elisha Johnson for President, Mrs. H. Montgomery, Vice

President, Mrs. W. Pitkin, Secretary, and Mrs. T. H. Rochester, Treasurer.

The first efforts of the society were directed to providing missionary services in parts adjacent, as is evident from the following extract from a letter of Mr. Cuming, dated May 21, 1827, enclosing to his correspondent a copy of the constitution of the newly-formed society:

"The inducements which the society can at present hold out are by no means so great as we wish we had it in our power to offer. But when it is mentioned that there are strong, very strong reasons to authorize the belief that the prudent, zealous, persevering efforts of some able and pious clergyman would much promote the interests of the Episcopal Church in this quarter and result in building up two or three respectable congregations, we think we present an argument calculated to have much weight with those who sincerely love the Church."

The minutes of the society show that appropriations were made from time to time for missionary work at Penfield, Pittsford, Brockport, Scottsville, and Honeoye Falls. The need of missionary work within the city (for Rochester became a city in 1834) claimed more and more attention, and from 1846 (with increased ability on the part of diocesan agencies to care for outlying points), this society addressed its efforts

mainly to the city field by providing successive
Rectors with clerical assistance. With some
modification of its name, the society remained
in existence till Feb. 3, 1868, when the Christian
activity of the ladies was directed into other
channels. It may here, however, be fitly re-
marked that great interest was early manifested
by the congregation in the missionary cause,
both foreign and domestic; an interest largely
fostered by this association, which through
systematic annual offerings liberally contributed
to missionary objects. An evidence of the
special interest felt in the mission to Greece
lies in the fact that a scholarship in Dr. and
and Mrs. Hill's school at Athens was supported
by ladies in St. Luke's; and the first Greek
girl received into that school, Agathoula by
name, testified her gratitude by working on
canvas, with emblematical and ornamental designs, a scripture text, "In memoriam of Mrs.
Sophia Rochester, Dec. 9th, 1845"—a memento
still preserved in the Rochester family.

Another organization was formed of unmar-
ried ladies in the parish, on Ash Wednesday,
1827, to be known as "The Young Ladies'
Benevolent and Reading Society." Its objects were "to promote the mutual instruction
of the members, and to procure funds for charitable or religious purposes." The society

met once in two weeks, and during a reading
by one of their number, the others were required " industriously to employ themselves in
making such articles as may be disposed of to
the advantage of the society." Its benefactions
took a wide range, including appropriations to
missions, theological students, parochial needs
and the maintenance of a charity school ; and
its good work as a distinct organization was
continued until 1838.

The earlier establishment of the Rochester
Female Charitable Society, Feb. 26, 1822, should
also properly be noted here ; which, although
a general organization, included among its first
officers and members many ladies of promin-
ence in St. Luke's Church. The first public
discourse in its behalf was preached by the
Rector of St. Luke's, and it has ever retained
the confidence and practical sympathy of the
congregation.

The letter of Rev. Mr. Cuming last quoted
contains, at the close, the following important
reference : " Measures are now taking to organize another Episcopal congregation in this village, next Monday." The measures referred to
originated in the following action of the Vestry
of St. Luke's, May 7, 1827 :

" WHEREAS, The congregation of St. Luke's
has become so numerous in consequence of the

increasing population of the village, that their present church cannot afford the necessary accommodation, and it being therefore advisable to establish an additional church in the Village of Rochester, and application having been made by parishioners of St. Luke's Church residing on the east side of the Genesee river for the organization of such additional church and society agreeably to the Constitution and Canons of the Protestant Episcopal Church ; therefore,

Resolved, That the said additional church be located on the east side of the Genesee river within the bounds of the village corporation.

Resolved, That a committee of five be appointed to carry the above resolutions into effect in a legal manner and as soon as practicable, and that the following gentlemen compose said committee : Messrs. Atkinson, Johnson, Boulton, Whittlesey and Pitkin.

Resolved, That the said committee wait upon the Rev. Mr. Cuming and express to him the continued confidence and attachment of all the parishioners of St. Luke's Church, and request him to proceed in the organization of the additional church."

In accordance with this action, St. Paul's Church was organized, May 28, 1827, and the following communicants dismissed from St.

Luke's to the new parish: Mr. and Mrs. Wm.
Atkinson, Mr. and Mrs. Samuel J. Andrews,
Mr. and Mrs. Jared N. Stebbins, Giles Boulton,
E. Smith Lee, Mrs. Susan Lee, Mrs. Mary
Williams, Mrs. Elisha Johnson, John Carnes,
Mrs. Richard P. Petherick, and Mrs. W. G,
Russell. Five others also were dismissed dur-
ing the year to form the nucleus of a new
organization in the village of Penfield, to be
called Trinity Church.

A contract for a bell of 2,000 lbs. weight was
authorized to be made, July 5, 1827, with Ward,
Bartholomew & Brainerd. Its cost was $900,
$500 of which was provided by the proceeds of
a lot given to the parish for this purpose by
Colonel Fitzhugh. The bell was hung in the
tower, April 17, 1828.

At the Easter meeting in this year, Monday
in Easter week was substituted for Thursday as
the time of the annual election. An enlargement of the church by the addition of two
arches at the west end was deemed expedient,
which would increase its length by thirty feet.
A contract was entered into with Elias J.
Mershon to execute this plan at an expense of
$3,000, Wm. Pitkin, S. O. Smith and F. Whit-
tlesey being the building committee. The work
was so conducted that the use of the church
was not interrupted, and the new part was

thrown open for occupancy in the fall of the same year.

The Rectorship of the Rev. Mr. Cuming was brought to a close by his resignation under date March 23, 1829, after an incumbency of eight years and four months. The Vestry accepted the resignation, "deeply regretting the existence of reasons that in his estimation are deemed of sufficient weight and importance to determine him to resign a situation he has so usefully occupied and the duties of which he has so faithfully and satisfactorily discharged."

An invitation to become the Rector was now extended to the Rev. Francis L. Hawks of New Haven, but declined by him on the ground of duty to his present parish and the condition of his health.

The Rev. Henry J. Whitehouse of Reading, Pa., was then called to the Rectorship, Sept. 9, 1829. After visiting the parish and officiating, the call was renewed, Oct. 4, by the Vestry and accepted "by the advice of Bishop Hobart," and on the first Sunday in December the new Rector entered upon his duties. His formal Institution took place Aug. 29, 1830. The rite of confirmation was administered in the evening of the same day to sixty-one candidates; on which occasion the Bishop accidentally overturned the alabaster font, which was thus broken to pieces. It was his last service in St. Luke's, as his lamented death took place on the 12th of the ensuing month. The Vestry placed on record their feelings in reference to the loss of their beloved Bishop, in the following language : " But two weeks before his decease, he in this church instituted our Rector and administered the apostolic rite of confirmation. It was almost his last ministerial act. We feel sensibly, we hope, this divine dispensation, and humbly pray God to direct us in the way of our duty, and that in due time He will raise up another bishop who shall with equal consistency preserve the integrity of the Church, with equal self-devotedness dedicate himself to her interests, with equal purity adorn her highest office, and, like him we mourn, be the polished gentleman, the practical scholar, the consistent Christian and the best of bishops." The church was draped in black and the Vestry wore the usual badge of mourning, for thirty days.

The Rector reported to the Convention of this year, that he had given a third service for ten or twelve Sunday evenings in the village of Penfield, and occasionally a week-service in the town of Brighton. In the following year, these services in Penfield were continued, and six persons were confirmed there by Bishop Onderdonk, Aug. 22, 1831.

The venerable founder of the village and the first warden of the church, Col. Nathaniel Rochester, deceased on the 4th of May, 1831, at the age of seventy-nine years. The Vestry manifested their respect and affection for his memory by appropriate resolutions and official participation in the funeral solemnities. On that occasion a memorable sermon was preached by the Rector, from the text, Gen. xliii. 27, "The old man of whom ye spake, is he yet alive?"

A communication addressed to the Rev. Mr. Whitehouse by the Vestry of St. Paul's Church, bearing date Dec. 5, 1831, was laid by him before the Vestry of St. Luke's, in which it was unanimously proposed to associate the two Churches under his parochial charge as Rector of both, with authority to procure an assistant-minister,—the services and the expenses to be equally divided between the two Churches. The Vestry of St. Luke's, after full considera-tion of the subject, found themselves of one opinion as to the inadvisability of the proposed scheme, and to a detailed statement of their objections thereto, added these words: "This Vestry receive with much gratification the expression of the committee of St. Paul's to our Rector, of their 'approbation of the views and policy exhibited by him during his connec-

tion with St. Luke's Church,' and sincerely hope
it is an earnest of the desire and determination
of that congregation to be governed by the
same sound and consistent views and policy, as
they are calculated to present our episcopal
institutions under one form, establish harmony
and engage the cordial co-operation of the
members of our respective congregations."

In 1832, a building was erected in the rear
of the Church as a lecture-room and for the
Sunday School, and also for the Charity
School, which it was proposed to establish. This latter was organized in 1833 with
seventy-five scholars and was supported mainly
by the Young Ladies' Benevolent Society of St.
Luke's, Gershom P. Waldo and Ethan Allen,
both afterwards in Orders in the Church, being
among the teachers of the school. The subsequent development of the common school
system occasioned its discontinuance, and in
April, 1843, the Vestry authorized " the giving
away of the Charity School apparatus."

At a meeting of the Vestry, Sept. 29, 1832,
the embarrassed condition of the affairs of St.
Paul's Church were again presented to their
attention through a communication from the
Vestry of the latter, whereupon the following
preamble and resolutions were adopted :

" WHEREAS, certain statements of the affairs and condition of St. Paul Church in the Village of Rochester from the Vestry thereof, have been submitted to the consideration of the Vestry of this Church ; from which it appears that the pecuniary affairs of said Church are in a condition so embarrassed that they entertain no hope of being able to extricate themselves. and that without means, without a Rector and burdened with debt, they fear that they must sink under their difficulties, the Church be borne down, the congregation dispersed and the building sold, to the great injury of the Episcopal interest in this section, unless some new arrangement can be made for their relief and the benefit of the Church in general, and so suggesting that the Corporation of this Church should purchase the building of St. Paul's Church as a Chapel of St. Luke's, as the only practical measure of saving it from entire sacrifice and averting a serious and permanent injury to the prosperity of the Episcopal Church generally, therefore

Resolved, that the interests of the Episcopal Church demand that St. Luke's Church should make an effort to purchase the building known as St. Paul's Church as a Chapel of this Church. if it can be done without too great a burden upon its resources and funds.

Resolved, that the Rector of this Church be empowered to ascertain what foreign resources can be depended upon for the above object, and to this intent, if necessary, present the matter to the Vestry of Trinity Church, New York."

After considerable negotiation, it was finally deemed unwise and impracticable by the Vestry of St. Luke's for them to assume the responsibility which the purchase of St. Paul's as a Chapel would involve, since the conditions connected with the offer of Trinity Church, New York, to pay the interest on $10,000 indebtedness for two years, required the purchase of the property by St. Luke's and the clearing off of all claims and incumbrances in excess of that amount.

A plan for the reorganization of St. Paul's under another name was subsequently devised, and liberally aided by Trinity Church, New York ; and the new corporation of Grace Church came, through foreclosure, into possession of the property.

The only occasion when St. Luke's has been visited by fire was in the early morning of Sunday, December 23, 1832, when the damage was slight and mainly by water. The kind invitation of their neighbors of the First Presbyterian

Society to worship in their edifice was gratefully accepted: which courtesy the Vestry were pleased to reciprocate on a subsequent occasion, when the walls of the First Church came to be considered unsafe; proffering the use of the Church to a religious society, whose relations with St. Luke's, its oldest and nearest neighbor, have always been of the most friendly character.

The Rev. Mr. Whitehouse proposing a trip to Europe for his health, and the Vestry expressing their cordial concurrence in the plan, he left the city Aug. 8, 1833, having preached a farewell sermon on the evening preceding. The Rev. James A. Bolles, of New York, was invited by the Vestry "to take charge of the parish as assistant minister thereof from the first day of September next at a salary of $600. The Rev. Mr. Bolles accepted the proposition, preaching his first sermon Sept. 15. The Rector returned Dec. 7, 1834, having received during his absence the honorary degree of Doctor of Divinity from Geneva College.

In 1836 a project for the establishment of a second offshoot of St. Luke's was agitated, and a committee of the Vestry was appointed to "circulate a subscription for purchasing a lot for a new church in Frankfort." As the result of this effort an eligible site was secured oppo-

4

site Brown's Square, and Seth C. Jones opened
a Sunday School in the school-house which then
stood on the square; and here the work rested
for a time.

In October of the same year the Rev. Dr.
Whitehouse, having secured leave of absence
from his duties, was married in New York and
sailed for Europe Nov. 22, remaining abroad
until Oct. 8, 1837. The services meanwhile
were supplied by the Rev. N. F. Bruce, M. D.

Toward the close of the year 1843, $1200 was
subscribed " for the purpose of making necessary and suitable repairs on or about the exter-
ior of the church edifice and for erecting chancel rail, alteration in gallery, cleaning and
painting ceiling and walls, varnishing wood-
work, carpeting aisles, procuring trimmings for
desk and pulpit, etc." The desk and pulpit
therefore were themselves constructed at an
earlier date, as is further evidenced by a parch-
ment recently found attached to the interior of
the pulpit, on which is inscribed in the hand-
writing of Dr. Whitehouse and bearing date
June 29, 1839, " This pulpit was erected A. D.
1836 from original designs of the Rev. Henry
J. Whitehouse, D. D., Thomas Thorn, carpenter.   The Screen and Canopy, completed 1839,
from designs by the same, Elijah Somers and

Henry Rogers, carpenters; Painting and Grain-
ing by Wm. H. Myers."

The ministry of Dr. Whitehouse was terminated by his resignation Feb. 19, 1844, his farewell sermon being preached on the 5th of the
ensuing May. The Vestry and congregation
very unwillingly assented to the separation of
the ties which had bound them together for
fourteen years and five months, and placed on
record their testimony to his ability and fidelity, and their recognition of the fact that to
his faithful services it was chiefly due that the
Church which he " found comparatively feeble "
he was leaving " strong, prosperous and influential."

A call to the vacant rectorship was extended,
May 9, 1844, to the Rev. Thomas C. Pitkin, of
Louisville, Ky., and accepted by him May 21st.
He entered upon his duties July 14, 1844, just
27 years from the date of the parish organization, and was instituted by Bishop DeLancey on
the 11th of the following August.

The influence of the new Rector was cordially given to the realization of the project to
establish a new church in the northern part of
the city. The friends of the movement and the
subscribers to the lot already secured on
Brown's Square, met in August, 1845, in the
public school house corner of Fish (now Centre)

and Jones Sts., and inaugurated public service
Sunday afternoons and evenings under the
auspices of the Rector. This movement resulted in the formal organization, Oct. 27, of
Trinity Church. The Rev. Vandervoort Bruce
was elected the first Rector, and it was resolved
to sell the lot on Brown's Square, as being
rather too far out of the city, and to purchase
one which was regarded as more eligible on the
corner of Fish and Frank Sts.

The Rev. Mr. Pitkin " finding his health inadequate to the care of so large a parish," tendered his resignation April 3, 1847, which took
effect after three years of service, on the 12th
of the following July, amid general expressions
of regret on the part of the people. He was
assisted during part of the year 1846, by the
Rev. John N. Norton. An invitation to the
Rectorship was now extended to the Rev. Wm.
Suddards, of Philadelphia, but declined by him.

The charge of the Parish was then committed
temporarily to the Rev. T. F. Wardwell, who
officiated from Aug. 29, till the close of the
year, when the Rev. Henry W. Lee, of Springfield, Mass., who had been called to the Rectorship, October 18, entered upon his duties
January 2, 1848. He was instituted by Bishop
DeLancey, Feb. 16, 1848. In his onerous pastoral labors in the parish, he was successively

assisted by the Revs. Edw. Meyer, Geo. H. McKnight, Bethel Judd, D. D., W. H. Barris, Geo. N. Cheney, Geo. W. Watson and Theodore A. Hopkins; funds for that purpose being provided in part by the Ladies' Missionary Society. Services were frequently held in the suburbs of the City, and in the town of Brighton.

During the year 1848, the sum of $4,000 was subscribed to liquidate a standing indebtedness of the corporation. The debt was accordingly canceled upon payment of the amount pledged and report thereof made to the Vestry Aug. 5, 1850.

A proposition to introduce gas into the Church was negatived June 4, 1849; which improvement was not effected till Dec. 24, 1853.

A committee appointed to circulate a subscription to provide a chime of bells and a new organ, consisting of Messrs. Kidd, Pitkin, Churchill, Dewey and Whittlesey, reported July 1, 1850, that they had secured $3,600; whereupon contracts were authorized to be made with A. Meneely, of Troy, for the chimes, and with Appleton & Warren for the new organ.

At the first Commencement of the University of Rochester, June 9, 1851, the honorary

degree of Doctor of Divinity was conferred
upon the Rev. Mr. Lee.

In April, 1854, on the retirement of Mr. and
Mrs. D. M. Dewey from the choir, the Vestry
expressed their cordial thanks for their faithful
and valuable services, rendered gratuitously for
upwards of sixteen years. A similar resolution,
accompanied by a valuable testimonial, had
been voted by the Vestry in December, 1845.
Besides Mrs. Dewey, her sisters, Mrs. J. M.
Winslow and Mrs. Albert Walker, had previously rendered efficient and acceptable services in the choir for many years. The
resignation of Dr. Lee, after a ministry of
seven years, occasioned by his election to the
Episcopate of Iowa, was presented Oct. 9, 1854,
and accepted with "unmingled feelings of
regret and with grateful appreciation of the
many qualities which have rendered his ministry so important to the prosperity of our parish,
and which have endeared him to the people of
his charge."

His Consecration as Bishop of Iowa took
place in St. Luke's, on the 18th of Oct., 1854,
Bishop J. H. Hopkins presiding, and Bishop
Manton Eastburn preaching the sermon,
Bishops McCoskry, DeLancey, Burgess and
Whitehouse uniting in the imposition of hands.
His first episcopal act was the Confirmation of

a class of thirty-five, in his own Church, on the 24th of December.

The Vestry meanwhile had called to the Rectorship the Rev. Benjamin Watson, of Zion Church, Newport, R. I., who accepted the same and entered upon his duties April 29, 1855, the services during the interim having been maintained by the Rev. T. A. Hopkins, assistant minister at the close of the last rectorate.

The necessity of a fourth Episcopal Church, which had been increasingly felt, resulted in the organization of a new parish in the southeast quarter of the city. The first official act of the new Rector was to officiate, at an early hour on the 29th of April, in Palmer's Hall, at the primary service of the new congregation, mainly composed of parishioners of St. Luke's. From this beginning sprung the important and prosperous parish of Christ Church.

The Institution of the Rev. Mr. Watson, by Bishop DeLancey, took place on Thursday. Feb. 14, 1856.

During the first year of his ministry, the church edifice was thoroughly repaired within and without, at an expense of over $5,000. The subscription to defray this improvement being some $1,500 short of that amount, the Vestry saw fit to mortgage the church. It was at this time that the present stained glass was inserted in the windows, the interior frescoed and the tower remodeled. Largely increased expense was also incurred for music. An ineffectual effort was made in April, 1859, to procure a rectory, but the realization of its importance bore fruit a few years later.

The Rev. Mr. Watson, finding the climate uncongenial, and having been called to the Church of the Atonement, Philadelphia, presented his resignation, which was regretfully accepted, July 23, 1859, to take effect the 7th of the following month, when he delivered his farewell discourse; it being recorded that "during his term of four years and three month's service as our Rector, he has, by his ability, fidelity and exemplary Christian deportment in the discharge of his arduous duties, won the respect, confidence and affection of his whole congregation." His assistants were the Revs. Robt. W. Lewis and Chas. E. Cheney. The services during the interim were supplied by the Rev. W. B. Otis, from Aug. 7 to Oct. 2, 1859.

The Rev. R. Bethell Claxton, D. D., of St. Paul's Church, Cleveland, O., was called to the Rectorship, Oct. 1, 1859, and entered upon his duties on the 1st of the following December. On the 20th of February ensuing, he was

instituted by Bishop DeLancey, Bishop H. W.
Lee preaching the sermon.

Steps were efficiently taken by the Vestry to
secure a rectory, and a negotiation to obtain
property on Fitzhugh street was terminated by
an authorization to purchase, Aug. 25, 1860, at
the price of $7,000, of which $4,000 was paid
in cash.

The patriotic spirit of the congregation manifested itself, April 29, 1861, in a resolution of
the Vestry to procure the National colors and
erect a flag-staff on the church, and also to present a Prayer-Book to every volunteer from the
City of Rochester, who would accept it. The
flag was raised on the tower of the church on
the 4th of May; on which occasions addresses
were made to a large concourse of people by
the Rector, Hon. Alfred Ely and Roswell
Hart, Esq.

The plan of building a Mission Chapel was
at several meetings urged by the Rector upon
the Vestry without eliciting from that body
any satisfactory encouragement; but convinced
of the necessity of such provision for those at
a distance from the church, he persevered in
his design and succeeded in founding the
Chapel of the Good Shepherd, in the eleventh
ward,—a part of the city at that time destitute
of all religious privileges. The means to ac-

complish this result were provided by the Sunday-school, the Ladies' Missionary Society and a few willing helpers. The corner-stone of a neat edifice of brick, 28 x 52, with a porch 8 feet square, upon a lot 54 x 150, was laid, by the Rector, Sept. 23, 1863; and on the 31st of July in the next year, he had the happiness of opening the Chapel for Divine Service. The total cost of the building was upwards of $3,000.

As early as June, 1861, the Rev. Dr. Claxton addressed a communication to the Vestry, proposing the establishment of "an Asylum for orphans and destitute children, to be under the especial care of our Church in Rochester." The Vestry declined to take action in the matter; but the nucleus of a fund to establish such an institution was formed by the collections at the joint-service of the several parishes on successive Maundy Thursdays, beginning in 1861.

Plans and elevations for a new church edifice were presented to the Vestry by Mr. William Churchill, Feb. 24, 1864, and a committee was appointed to "ascertain if money can be raised for the erection of a new church," and "to present to pew-owners a request to surrender their pews in the church." This committee subsequently reported that they "had not succeeded in inducing pew-holders to surrender their pews or to submit to new annuities."

In the failure of the project to build a new church, it was decided, April 11, 1864, to erect a very much needed Sunday School building, and Messrs. Bronson, Brewster and Hawley were appointed to act in the matter. The contract for the work, however, was not formally authorized until April 24, 1865, when $2.700 had been collected for the purpose, nor finally completed till April, 1866, at a total cost for building and furniture of $6,000.

The inadequacy of the income of the Church to meet its current expenses without continual resort to special subscriptions, pressed so heavily upon the Vestry that in the Spring of 1864, they called a meeting of the congregation and presented as the root of the difficulty their inability legally to fix such annuities upon the pews as would be sufficient to defray the expenses of the Church, and earnestly requesting the pew-owners to relinquish their leases, which limited the amount which each could be required to pay : but strenuous effort on the part of the Vestry failed to secure the surrender of the vested rights.

A plan however was subsequently devised, to which all the pew-holders except two assented, by which the Vestry were to extinguish the rights of such lessees as would not surrender their pews for a term of years by the payment

of a consideration ; and the Church was ordered
to be mortgaged for $6,000 to procure the nec
essary funds, after paying the existing mortgage
debt of $1,200 and advances by the Treasurer,
amounting to $1,700. Application was also
ordered to be made to the Legislature for
the passage of an act authorizing the Vestry
to assess upon pews and sittings the current
expenses of the corporation.

The laborious duty of securing the surrender
of 27 leases and the extinguishment by purchase
of 14 others devolved upon Mr. T. C. Montgomery, to whom the church is under lasting
obligations in this matter, as well as for another
most important service in perfecting an absolute title to the church property through
releases secured by him from the heirs of Rochester, Fitzhugh and Carroll.

It having been proposed to invite the newly-
elected Assistant Bishop of the Diocese to make
Rochester his residence, the Vestry appointed
a committee to confer with committees from
the other parishes in the city on the subject.
As the result of such conference, steps were
taken to provide by general subscription a
home for Bishop Coxe in this city, but he ulti-
mately decided it to be for the best interests of
the Diocese that he should reside in Buffalo.

The Rev. Dr. Claxton having been appointed

" Professor of Pulpit Eloquence and Pastoral Care" in the Philadelphia Divinity School, presented his resignation to take effect Oct. 1, 1865 ; in accepting which, the Vestry "bear willing testimony to the fidelity with which he ministered in holy things, the purity of his doctrines, the earnestness and ability of his pulpit appeals, the untiring industry and self-denying zeal which has marked the discharge of his parochial duties and the uniform interest and affection with which he has watched over the flock." During Dr. Claxton's ministry of five years and ten months, he was assisted by the Revs. Joseph Kidder, Fred. N. Luson, DeWitt C. Loop, Fred. M. Gray and Horatio Gray.

Upon the nomination of the retiring Rector, the Rev. Wm. J. Clark was placed in charge of the parish from Oct. 1, 1865, which engagement terminated April 18, 1866.

The Rev. Henry C. Potter, D. D., of St. John's Church, Troy, was invited, Nov. 8, 1865, to accept the rectorship, but though earnestly urged on the occasion of a personal visitation to the parish to accept the charge, he after careful deliberation declined the call.

A joint committee of three from the Vestry and three from the congregation on the subject of securing a Rector, recommended, April 9, 1866, that an engagement be made with the

5

Rev. Henry Anstice, officiating at St. Barnabas' Church, Irvington, to take pastoral charge
of the parish for one year; and a special committee consisting of N. T. Rochester, T. C.
Montgomery and Aaron Erickson was appointed
to extend the invitation. At a subsequent
meeting the committee reported "that they
could not make any arrangement with the Rev.
Henry Anstice to take temporary charge of
this parish." A call to the Rectorship at a salary of $2,000, with the use of the Rectory and
$800 for an assistant was thereupon extended
April 23, 1866, and accepted to take effect on
the 13th of the following month.

At the first meeting of the Vestry with the
new Rector, he was requested to take the keys
of the Chapel of the Good Shepherd and to
make such disposition thereof as he with the
concurrence of the Vestry may from time to
time think advisable," and in accordance with a
subsequent resolution he received and accepted
the title to the property from the Rev. Dr.
Claxton, the Vestry having been unwilling to
assume the legal responsibility incident thereto.

A plan for general city mission work having
been projected by Mr. George R. Clark and the
Rev. Dr. Van Ingen under the name of " The
St. Matthew's Church Mission," and it having
been intimated to the Vestry that the said Mis-

sion was desirous of purchasing the Good Shepherd Chapel in order to unify the work of
Church extension in the city under one management, it was resolved "with a view to promote harmony of feeling and action between
the several clergy and parishes of Rochester
and as an expression of interest in the newly
inaugurated joint mission work," to enter into
a contract to convey the property to trustees
for the use of the said mission. The " St. Matthew's Mission " accordingly conducted services
in the chapel as well as at other points in the city
by its missionaries, the Rev. R. M. Duff, Dean,
and the Rev. E. S. Wilson, assisted by Mr. S.
D. Boorom and D. H. Lovejoy, M. D., candidates for Orders. Upon the dissolution of that
organization, however, in June, 1867, the chapel
reverted to St. Luke's and the services were
continued therein by the Rector and his assistants. The other points at which services had
been sustained by this joint missionary effort
were the school house near Deep Hollow, which
was committed to the care of Trinity Church;
the Oregon St. Mission, which was assigned
to Grace Church, and Hope Chapel, which
was committed to Christ Church, and developed
by the care of its Rector and some zealous laymen into St. Clement's in July, 1871.

The Vestry having had under consideration

the advisability of thoroughly remodeling and
refitting the interior of the church, and placing
the whole edifice in the best possible condition,
requested the Rector to call a meeting of the
congregation to express their views upon the
subject. At this meeting, held July 16, 1866,
plans and estimates were presented and dis-
cussed, and on motion of Mr. Aaron Erickson,
it was resolved, "That the congregation do
advise the Vestry to make the improvements
proposed, and at the same time to make provision for paying off the entire church debt
upon the basis of property in the pews." Steps
were, accordingly, at once taken to carry out
the recommendations of the congregation, and
Messrs Bronson, Brewster and Perkins, with the
Rector as chairman, were appointed the building committee, and the same members of the
Vestry, together with Mr. Erickson, and Hon.
E. D. Smith were designated a committee to
solicit subscriptions,—the labors of which latter
work, devolved almost entirely upon Judge
E. D. Smith and Mr. G. H. Perkins.

The last service in the old church, prior to
its occupation by the workmen, was held Oct.
7, 1866 ; from which time the congregation wor-
shiped statedly on Sunday afternoons in the
First Presbyterian Church, opposite, which had
been kindly tendered for that purpose by the

Christian courtesy of its Trustees. A Wednesday evening service with lectures on the Prayer Book was also held in our Sunday School building, and the sessions of the Sunday School were not interrupted.

The Rev. M. R. St. J. Dillon-Lee entered upon his duties as the first assistant to the Rector, Sept. 2, '66. With his co-operation weekly cottage services were maintained throughout the Winter in the 8th Ward, and a Sunday afternoon service established in the following Spring in a building rented for that purpose. The whole southwestern section of the city was divided into districts, and lady visitors assigned to each with a view to organized personal ministries of divers sorts to the people there resident.

The committee of the Vestry which had been appointed in April to act with similar committees from the other three parishes for the purpose of purchasing a lot in Mt. Hope Cemetery for the interment of "persons attached to the Episcopal Church for whose burial no other appropriate place should be provided," reported Jan. 31, '67, that they had purchased jointly such a lot for $324, of which $106 was to be paid by St. Luke's.

The work of repair was meanwhile slowly

progressing in the church building. It had
been found necessary to make excavations,
build foundations for the pillars, put in new
timbers and flooring and make unplanned alter-
ations and improvements to such an extent that
the work was protracted into the short days of
Winter and the expense very materially increased. Before the re-modeling of the edifice
there was no middle aisle and no entrance
through the tower; the pews had doors as high
as the backs of the seats; there were square pews
in the gallery, and the building was heated with
stoves. Steam-heating apparatus was now introduced throughout the church and Sunday School
building, and the organ was renovated and its
power increased by the addition of several stops.
On the 10th of March, 1867, the church was re-
opened for Divine Service by the Bishop of the
Diocese, and on the 14th inst. in the presence of
all the city clergy the formal Institution of the
Rector took place; Dr. T. C. Pitkin of Buffalo
and Dr. Abner Jackson of Geneva, acting as
attending presbyters, Bishop Coxe preaching the
sermon and performing the ceremony, and William Pitkin, Esq., presenting the keys of the
church,—an office he had discharged at the
Institution of each preceding Rector; all of
them except the first having been formally
instituted into the Rectorship.

A statement of the financial condition of the parish was laid before the congregation on Easter Monday, April 22, 1867, from which it appeared that there had been expended in repairing the church edifice about $19,000, and that the sums collected from subscriptions and sales of pews amounted to $18,770, with about $7,000 more due and unpaid. The debts of the Church, contracted before the repairs were commenced, were stated at $6,000 on the church building, $3,000 of purchase money on the Rectory, $2,400 in contracts for purchase of Exchange St. property in rear of Rectory, and $1,000 balance due and and unpaid on the Sunday School building; thus showing the total debt of the corporation, before the improvements were begun, to have been $12,400. The hope which had been entertained, that the entire debt would be paid off at this time was therefore disappointed. A material reduction of it, however, was effected through the gradual collection of unpaid subscriptions, proceeds of sales of pews, and the operation of a sinking fund created by the excess of current income over expenses: so that before the meeting of the Convention in August, 1867, not only had the entire cost of the improvements been defrayed, but $3,200 had been paid upon the outstanding obligations, and the mortgage on the church was still further reduced by $1,000, within three years thereafter.

The parochial activity in City Mission work was at this time approaching its highest development. An additional Assistant Minister was needed to devote himself particularly to the work at the Good Shepherd ; and provision having been made therefor, the Rev. Jacob Miller entered upon his duties in that field in July, 1867. In the 8th Ward, the services were attended with deep interest, and the people of the district showed themselves in earnest for the erection of a chapel by subscribing $1,000 for that purpose. Service on Sunday afternoons and a Sunday School were maintained in the school house on Lake Ave., near Deep Hollow, from July, 1867, when this enterprise which had been a legacy to him from St. Matthew's Church Mission, was committed by the Rector of Trinity to the Rector of St. Luke's. In the Ontario St. neighborhood, cottage services were well attended by the people in that locality, and the duty of chaplain to the City Hospital was also discharged by one of our staff of clergy, Divine service being held for one year on every Lord's Day afternoon.

Meanwhile, the Rev. Mr. Dillon-Lee having accepted a position as assistant minister in Christ Church, New Orleans, resigned after thirteen months of service and was followed by the Rev. David H. Lovejoy, M. D., Sept. 29. 1867. who remained one year in the parish.

The 12th of March, 1868, marks the progress of the work at the Good Shepherd Chapel in the creation, by the Rector, of a quasi-Vestry, to relieve him of details and represent the needs and wishes of the people. The result of this arrangement was to rapidly develop the interest and self-sustaining power of the congregation, and pave the way for that ecclesiastical independence which was perfected a year later.

The corner-stone of the new chapel on Frances street was laid by the Rector in the absence of the Bishop, on the 23rd of July, 1868, addresses being delivered by the Revs. F. S. Rising, of New York, and J. H. Waterbury, of Le Roy. The completed building was formally opened for divine service Feb. 28. 1869. The total cost of the chapel was $10,000. which had been raised by subscriptions and five-cent collections, by the Sunday School, by a public lecture given by Bishop Lee, and from the proceeds of some lots on Penn street given to the Rector for this purpose by the heirs of Asa Sprague. The chapel was thus described in the "Gospel Messenger": "It is neatly and substantially built of brick, in Early English style, sixty feet by forty-two inside, slate-roofed

with four double lancet windows on each side
and a window in front on either side of a central
tower, which is eighty-two feet high. The in-
side walls are rough-finished, blocked and
stained. The seats are neatly upholstered in
crimson damask, having reversible backs for
Sunday School purposes, arranged in double
rows on each side of a central aisle, with side
aisles at the walls, and will accommodate three
hundred persons." Jonathan Dent was the
mason, Thomas Williamson the carpenter, and
Isaac Loomis the architect, by whom the chapel
was built.

On the 18th of Sept, 1868, the Bishop
advanced to the priesthood the two assistants
of the parish, the Revs. Jacob Miller and David
H. Lovejoy, M. D., presented by the Rector:
twenty clerical members of the Rochester Con-
vocation being present.

The independent organization of the Church
of the Good Shepherd was effected on the 29th
of March, in this year, and the Rev. J. Miller
was elected Rector. Forty-one families and
fifty-one communicants were transferred from
St. Luke's to form the nucleus of the new parish. And thus the Good Shepherd took its
place as the fourth daughter of St. Luke's
among the city Churches.

The corner-stone of the Church Home was

laid April 20, 1869, in the unavoidable absence of the Bishop, by the Rector of St. Luke's, who also made the address at the formal opening of the Institution, Oct. 26th, of the same year, all the city Rectors being present and taking part in the services.

The Rev. W. W. Raymond became assistant to the Rector, with special duties in the 8th Ward field, Feb. 7, 1869, and at the Ember Ordination, March 13, 1870, was advanced to the priesthood in Christ Church by Bishop Coxe, on presentation by the Rector of St. Luke's.

On the 8th of May, 1870, a morning service was instituted at the Epiphany, the name by which the chapel had been christened Nov. 7, 1869. Up to this time no sacrament had been administered in the chapel, but there was a Sunday School of 160 members and a stated congregation of 200 persons. A handsome font was now provided and a communion service. A better organ also was procured. A bell alone was lacking, and at Christmas-tide this want was also satisfactorily supplied.

The Rev. Mr. Raymond, after sixteen months of service in the parish, preached his last sermon May 22, 1870. The Rev. Geo. S. Baker came to take his place August, 14 of the same year.

During the summer of 1870, the Sunday

School building was thoroughly renovated, the walls painted, the woodwork oiled and the floor carpeted; the carpet being given as an individual contribution by one who delights to be liberal. In the following June the Vestry authorized a committee consisting of Jas. Brackett, C. F. Smith and Roswell Hart to repaint and decorate the interior of the church and build a new organ to replace the old, for which improvements $4,700 was raised by subscription. The total cost was $5,230.32, the balance being provided from the current revenue of the Church.

In Advent, 1871, the Rector organized the willing workers of the Church into a body known as the " Parochial Helpers." The District Visiting and Mothers' Meetings were especially effective in furthering the work in the 8th Ward, and were continued till the Chapel reached that stage in its development where labor of this sort more properly devolved on its own members. A Sewing School was also well sustained in the Epiphany. The sewing interest at the Mother-Church was known at this time by the name of the Industrial Circle; which, among its plentiful good works, provided for refurnishing the Vestry Room.

On the 19th of February, 1872, the Vestry authorized a committee with the Rector as chairman, to remove the old rectory to the

south side of the lot which it occupied and procure plans for the erection of a new and more
suitable residence for the Rector. The old rectory was accordingly removed and placed in
good order at an expense of $1,949.40; where-
upon the committee was authorized to proceed
with the erection of a new building not to exceed $12,000 in cost.

During the same summer a parsonage house
was erected on the lot adjoining the Epiphany,
at an expenditure of $4,000, while the chapel
itself was renovated and walls and woodwork
tastefully repainted.

The Rev. Wm. Long entered on his duties as
assistant to the Rector Dec. 1, 1872, remaining
in the parish four years and five months, until
April 29, 1877.

The new rectory being completed on the 12th
of April, 1873, a final report was made to the
Vestry by which it appeared that its cost had
been $11,961.69, and that this sum had been
provided by the sale of the old rectory and the
proceeds of a bank loan upon the new, in anticipation of the sale of the lots in the rear. A
new bell was this Spring hung in the tower at
a cost of $600, to replace its predecessor, which
had become useless.

On the 13th of April, 1874, Messrs. Brackett,
Perkins, Hart, Eastwood and Whittlesey were
6

appointed to solicit subscriptions to clear off the balance of the original debt on church and rectory, contracted in 1860 and 1864. An amount sufficient to extinguish this balance, $7,000, was raised within two months.

A service for deaf mutes was at this time inaugurated in one of the rooms of the Sunday School building, which has since been uninterruptedly continued on Sunday afternoons by Mr. J. C. Acker as lay-reader.

The need of some new missionary enterprise in the northern portion of the city being apparent, the Rector of St. Luke's, at the instance of the Bishop and with the concurrence of all the west-side clergy, took measures to establish a service and Sunday School under the name of St. John's Chapel on State St. A hall in Cochrane's block was secured and neatly fitted up at an expense of $600 for the opening service, Jan. 24, 1875, the Rev. J. J. Landers assisting. The Rector himself officiated every evening during the summer, but his personal connection with the enterprise ceased in September, and Mr. Landers conducted its affairs until the following February, when at the instance of the local clergy, and in view of the fact that a new Rector had infused fresh life into Trinity parish, and upon the distinct pledge of the Vestry of Trinity that they would occupy the field, the

Bishop advised the discontinuance of the mission. The Rev. Mr. Walsh at once took charge of the Sunday School and maintained a service, and the Vestry of Trinity redeemed its pledge at a later date in the removal of their Parish Church.

During this Summer of 1875, the Rector held missionary services in Fairport and Penfield on alternate Sunday afternoons for the benefit of the few Church people residing in those villages.

The Rev. Geo. S. Baker after five years and more of faithful service, resigned to accept the rectorship of St. James' Church, Batavia, in October, 1875. He was followed at once by the Rev. C. M. Nickerson, who became assistant minister on the 1st of November.

On the 13th of Sept., 1876, the Rev. Dr. Anstice organized the congregation of the Epiphany into an independent parish, and on his nomination the Rev. Chas. M. Nickerson was elected the first Rector. He transferred 170 families and 202 communicants to constitute the new parish, and deeded the property, consisting of the church and rectory, worth over $18,000, with a debt only upon the latter, to the newly organized corporation; which thus entered upon its independent life under most propitious auspices.

An ordination of special interest, from the fact that the candidate was one who had been baptized and confirmed in St. Luke's, was held June 11, 1876, when the Bishop conferred Deacons' Orders upon Mr. John W. Greenwood.

The Woman's Missionary Association, which had been organized in January, 1873, entered upon a career of increased efficiency in the fall of 1877, and has since continued weekly meetings during the working season, largely increasing the parish contributions for missions and gladdening many a missionary's heart by timely gifts of " boxes."

The Vestry appointed, Nov. 13, 1877, Messrs. Reynolds, Brackett and Wolcott "to solicit subscriptions to defray extraordinary expenses incurred by reason of necessary repairs to the church building and taxation for local improvements." Mr. Brackett, from this committee, reported Feb. 27, 1878, that they had raised about $2,150 for the purposes named.

In the winter of 1878, a sewing school was established at the church, with seventeen officers and 125 learners, which has since continued its sessions each winter. A series of " Mothers' Meetings" was also inaugurated, Oct. 18, which have proved productive of much blessing. A Guild, too, was organized which signalized the first year of its existence by raising means sufficient, together with the proceeds of two collections in the church, to re-carpet the building and make some improvements in the organ; which work was completed in the summer of 1879.

The 21st of December, 1879, was the occasion of another ordination of special interest. Byron Holley, Jr., a son of St. Luke's, was presented to the Bishop by the Rector, for admission to the Diaconate. He at once entered upon his duties as assistant minister, which position he held until called to take charge of the Church of the Good Shepherd, April 1, 1881.

The Vestry, on the 21st of May, 1880, resolved as follows: "That this Vestry, having heard of the proposed removal of Trinity Church to a new location in the north part of the city, hereby tender their sincere congratulations to the Rector and people of Trinity Church upon their brightened prospect of increased usefulness, and desire to express the earnest hope that a new era of prosperity is about to dawn upon them in their new and enlarged field."

" This corporation cordially invite the Rector and congregation of Trinity Church, pending the erection of their new edifice, to unite in worshiping with the congregation of St. Luke's under such arrangements as may be agreed upon by the Rectors."

During the winter of 1881-82, the Rector was
maturing plans for the consolidation of all the
agencies for good in the parish into one organization, intending to add several new departments of church work. Those plans culminated
in the organization of St. Luke's Guild, em-
bracing nine chapters, a full account of which,
with the names of the members of each Chapter, was published in a neat pamphlet at Easter,
1882. The object of the Guild is to co-operate
with the Rector in systematizing and develop-
ing the Christian activity of the parish.

Its membership consists of such persons as
may signify to the Rector their willingness and
determination to consecrate some portion of
their time and energy to such Church work as
shall be undertaken by the Guild. Its work is
divided into various departments, and is committed to the several Chapters of the Guild as
follows:

The work of the Sunday School Chapter is
to aid the Rector in the instruction of the
young people of the Parish in Biblical learning
and the doctrines of the Church.

The work of the Woman's Missionary Chapter is to awaken and develop the Missionary
Spirit, to diffuse intelligence regarding the several departments of the Church's Missionary
work, and to promote a personal devotion to

the cause in labor, prayer and systematic giving.

The work of the Choir Chapter is to render the "Service of Song in the House of the Lord" during the Lenten Season, and upon Holy-days and such other occasions of public worship as may be required.

The work of the Church Home Chapter is to promote the interests of this Institution by personal service and influence, and to carry into effect approved plans for raising funds for its support.

The work of the Mothers' Meeting Chapter is to carry on, by approved methods, that scheme of Christian effort known under this name, including religious and other instruction at the weekly social gathering, and the systematic visiting of the attendants upon the meetings, with personal ministries in their homes.

The work of the Sewing School Chapter is to organize and instruct classes of young girls in various kinds of useful and ornamental needle work.

The work of the Visitors' Chapter is to manifest a kindly interest in such of the sick and needy as may from time to time be commended to its care, to visit statedly the inmates of the Church Home and the City Hospital, and to prosecute the labor of love known as the Flower Mission.

The work of the Sanctuary Chapter is "the oversight of them that keep the charge of the sanctuary," the special care of the chancel, vestry room and vestments, the extension of the Church's hospitality to strangers on all occasions of public worship, and the arrangement through committees for the fit decoration of the Lord's House at Christmas and Easter.

The work of the Girls' Friendly Society Chapter is to seek out and bring into personal relations with the members of the Chapter, and with each other, such young women earning an independent livelihood as may be willing to associate themselves together in the bonds of friendliness, for mutual culture and interest in each other's welfare.

The general officers of the Guild, together with the Heads of Chapters, appointed by the Rector, and one representative selected by each Chapter, constitute the Guild Council, which meets bi-monthly, or otherwise as it may determine, for review of the work of the organization, consultation upon plans for its extension and increased efficiency, consideration of the Guild finances, appropriation of funds to the several Chapters, and the decision of any questions which may arise respecting the conduct of any department of the Guild work.

The Guild continues in efficient and successful operation, and is productive of much good.

During the present summer a new roof has

been placed on the Sunday School building, a larger boiler been substituted for the old in connection with the steam heating apparatus, which has been thoroughly overhauled, and other pairs effected at a cost of $1,200.

St. Luke's has always been a "pewed church." Its current income for the year ending Sept. 1, 1883 (to which date all the statistics and statements in this book are made up) is $7,811.48.

The harmony and prosperity which reign in the old mother-parish of St. Luke's leaves nothing in these respects to be desired.

The present officers of the Church are:

RECTOR,
Rev. Henry Anstice, D. D.

WARDENS,
Hon. E. D. Smith,   Gilman H. Perkins.

VESTRYMEN,
Hon. James Brackett,   Wm. Eastwood.
Joseph A. Eastman.   Clinton Rogers.
Edw. W. Williams,   Lorenzo Kelly.
Henry B. Hathaway,   Hon. Alfred Ely.

CLERK OF VESTRY,
Joseph A. Eastman.

TREASURER,
John H. Rochester.

Officers of the Church.

Rectors.

THE REV. FRANCIS H. CUMING, D. D.
Eight years and four months.
From Dec. 1, 1820, to April 1, 1829.

THE RT. REV. HENRY J. WHITEHOUSE, D. D., LL. D.
Fourteen years and five months.
From Dec. 6, 1829, to May 5, 1844.

THE REV. THOMAS C. PITKIN, D. D.
Three years.
From July 14, 1844, to July 12, 1847.

THE RT. REV. HENRY W. LEE, D. D., LL. D.
Seven years.
From Jan. 1, 1848, to Jan. 1, 1855.

THE REV. BENJAMIN WATSON, D. D.
Four years and three months.
From April 29, 1855, to Aug. 7, 1859.

THE REV. R. BETHELL CLAXTON, D. D.
Five years and ten months.
From Dec. 1, 1859, to Sept. 24, 1865.

THE REV. HENRY ANSTICE, D. D.
Seventeen years and four months
(to Sept., 1883).
From May 13, 1866.

Assistant Ministers.

UNDER REV. DR. WHITEHOUSE.
Rev. James A. Bolles,   Sept. 15. '33–Sept. 14, '34
Rev. N. F. Bruce, M. D.,   Nov. 6, '36–Nov. 1, '37

UNDER REV. DR. PITKIN.
Rev. John N. Norton,   April 26, '46–Nov. 22, '46

INTERIM.
Rev. T. F. Wardwell,   Aug. 29, '47–Jan. 1, '48

UNDER REV. DR. LEE.
Rev. Edward Meyer,   Rev. W. H. Barris,
Rev. Geo. H. McKnight, Rev. Geo. N. Cheney,
Rev. Bethel Judd, D.D., Rev. Geo. W. Watson,
        Rev. Theodore A. Hopkins.

INTERIM.
Rev. T. A. Hopkins,   Jan. 1, '55–May 1, '55

UNDER REV. DR. WATSON.
Rev. Robert W. Lewis, Rev. Charles E. Cheney.

INTERIM.
Rev. W. B. Otis,   Aug. 7, '59–Oct. 2, '59

UNDER REV. DR. CLAXTON.

Rev. Joseph Kidder,   May 1, '60–May 1, '61
Rev. Fred. N. Luson,   July 1, '61–Jan. 1, '62
Rev. DeWitt C. Loop,   March 1, '62–Sept. 1, '64
Rev. Fred. M. Gray,   Nov. 1, '64–Feb. 1, '65
Rev. Horatio Gray,   April 2, '65–July 2, '65

INTERIM.

Rev. W. J. Clark.   Oct. 1, '65–April 18, '66

UNDER REV. DR. ANSTICE.

Rev. M. R. St.J. Dillon, Sept. 2, '66–Sept. 22, '67
Rev. Jacob Miller,   July 7, '67–March 29, '69
Rev.D.H.Lovejoy,M.D.Sept. 29, '67–Sept. 20, '68
Rev. W. W. Raymond, Feb. 7, '69–May 22, '70
Rev. George S. Baker, Aug. 14, '70–Oct. 26, '75
Rev. William Long,   Dec. 1, '72–April 29, '77
Rev. J. J. Landers.   Jan. 24, '75–Sept. 5, '75
Rev. C. M. Nickerson, Nov. 1, '75–Sept. 13, '76
Rev. B. Holley, Jr.,   Dec. 21, '79–April 1, '81

Wardens.

Nathaniel Rochester,	1817-'19
Samuel J. Andrews,	1817-'19 & '21
George G. Sill,	1820
William Atkinson,	1820-'27
John Mastick,	1822-'26
William Pitkin,	1827-'65
Silas O. Smith,	1828-'33
Vincent Mathews,	1834-'46
N. T. Rochester,	1847-'58 & '66-'68
William Brewster,	1859-'72
Gilman H. Perkins,	1869-'83
E. Darwin Smith,	1873-'83

Vestrymen.

Roswell Babbit,	1817-'21
Silas O. Smith (W.),	1817-'27, '36, '40-'42 & '48
John Mastick (W.),	1817-'21
Lewis Jenkins,	1817-'19
John C. Rochester,	1817-'19
Elisha Johnson,	1817-'20 & '27
William Atkinson (W.),	1817-'19
Oliver Culver,	1817-'19
Augustine G. Dauby,	1820
Jared N. Stebbins,	1820-'21 & '27
S. Melancton Smith,	1820-'22
James H. Gregory,	1820-'22
Caleb L. Clark,	1821, '23, '24
John Swift,	1821
William W. Mumford,	1821-'22' & 24'-26
Jonathan Child,	1822, '24, '47 & '50-'53
William Pitkin (W.),	1822-'26
Solomon Cleveland,	1822, '24-'25 & '27
Elisha Taylor,	1822
Elisha B. Strong,	1823
John B. Elwood, M. D.,	1823
Thomas H. Rochester,	1823-'26, '32, '33 & '43
William P. Sherman,	1823
Thomas Kempshall,	1823
Burrage Smith,	1824, '25

Giles Boulton,	1825-'27
Frederick Whittlesey,	1826-'41, '44, '46, '47
Thomas Eggleston,	1828
Nathaniel T. Rochester (W.),	1828-'31 & '35-'38
John T. Talman,	1828-'33 & '42-'45
Henry Scrantom,	1828, '29, '45 & '49
Benjamin Seabury,	1828-'31
Joseph Field,	1829-'35 & '59-'65
Simeon Ford,	1830
Vincent Matthews (W.),	1831-'33
Walter White,	1832, '33
Matthew Mead,	1834-'41 & '45
Robert L. McCollum,	1834
Seth C. Jones,	1834-'45
John Haywood,	1834, '46, '48, '50, '51
John Allen,	1835-'42 & '45
William Brewster (W.),	1836-'38, '46, '47 & '50
David Hoyt,	1837-'44, '47 & '49
John Hawks,	1839-'43
Moses Dyer,	1839
Graham H. Chapin,	1842
Henry E. Rochester,	1843, '44
Jonathan King,	1843, & '53, '54
Darius Cole,	1843
William Kidd,	1844, '49-'50, & '55-'62
S. H. Packard,	1844
Rufus Keeler,	1845, '46, & '49-'51
E. Darwin Smith (W.),	1846, '47 & '69-'72
Ebenezer Watts,	1846-'48

Dellon M. Dewey,	1846, '48, '49
Andrew J. Brackett,	1847, '48
Thomas C. Montgomery,	1848, '53, '54, & '64–'66
Ebenezer Griffin,	1848,–'51, '54–'57 '59 & '60
Edward Whalen,	1848–'54, & '61, '62
N. B. Northrop,	1849
William Churchill,	1850, '51, & '62, '63
Joseph A. Eastman,	'51, '55–'61 '63, '64 & '79–'83
Aaron Erickson,	1851, & '62, '63
Azariah Boody,	1852, '53
Amon Bronson,	1852, & '61–'69
Joseph L. Lucas,	1852, '56, & '58–'61
Edward M. Smith,	1852
Chauncey Tucker,	1852
John Fairbanks,	1852, '53
Asa Sprague,	1853, '54
John Crombie,	1853, '54
Alfred Ely,	1854–'59, & '83
John E. Tompkins,	1854
Mortimer F. Reynolds,	1855, '77, & '79–'81
Francis Gorton,	1855, '56
Abram Karnes,	1855, & '63, '64
Frederick A. Whittlesey,	1855,–'62, & '74
Roswell Hart,	1856–'61, & '71–'83
John H. Rochester,	1857, '58
Martin S. Newton,	1857, & '67
Gilman H. Perkins (W.),	1858–61, & '66–'68
Edmund Lyon,	1862–'65
Nelson G. Hawley,	1862–'66

Paul W. Garfield,	1863, '64
Ebenezer E. Sill,	1865-'75
Thomas Hawks,	1865-'66
Edward A. Frost,	1865 & '67, '68
John P. Humphrey,	1866
R. Hart Rochester,	1866
George G. Munger,	1867, '68
Henry L. Churchill	1867-'69
Thomas Button,	1868, '69
Henry B. Hathaway,	1868 & '75-'83
James R. Chamberlin,	1869, '70 & '73-'75
Charles H. Chapin,	1869-'73
William Eastwood,	1869-'78, & '81-'83
James Brackett,	1870-'78 & '82, 83
Isaac H. Ruliffson,	1870
Edward W. Williams,	1870-'83
Thomas Raines,	1871
Charles F. Smith,	1871-'77
George P. Wolcott,	1876-'80
Clinton Rogers,	1878-'83
Mortimer C. Mordoff,	1878, '79
Lorenzo Kelly,	1881-'83

Clerks of the Vestry.

Roswell Babbit,	1817–'20
N. T. Rochester,	1821–32 & '35–'43
Henry E. Rochester,	Nov., 1832, '33 & '44
E. Darwin Smith,	1834
Thomas C. Montgomery,	1845–1854
Fred A. Whittlesey,	1855, '56, '62 & '74
Joseph A. Eastman,	1857, '61 & '79–'83
Paul W. Garfield,	1863–'65
Edward A. Frost,	1865 to Sept.
R. Hart Rochester,	Sept., 1865
John P. Humphrey,	1866 to Feb., '67
Allen Ayrault,	Feb., '67 to Apr., '67
Henry L. Churchill,	1867, '68
William Eastwood,	1869, '70
Thomas Raines,	1871
Charles F. Smith,	1872, '73
Edward P. Hart,	1875, '76
Edw. W. Williams,	1877, '78

Treasurers.

Roswell Babbit,	1817–'22
N. T. Rochester,	1823–Oct., '32
Wm. Pitkin,	Oct., '32–'36
F. Whittlesey,	1836–'39
Clarendon Morse,	Jan. 1840–'43
James M. Fish,	1844
Henry Scrantom,	1845–'48
Erasmus D. Smith,	June, 1848
Andrew J. Brackett,	Jan., 1849–'54
Edward Whalen,	1855–May, '62
Abram Karnes,	May, 1862–'64
E. R. Hammatt,	1865–'74
John H. Rochester,	1875–'83

Organists.

Daniel Clark,	1825–May, '27
William Staunton,	1827–May, '33
Mr. Randall,	May, '33–1834
Mr. Warner,	1834–1835
Israel P. Dana,	1835–April, '39
Marion S. McGregor,	April, 1839–Aug., '56
R. F. C. Ellis,	Aug., '56–Dec., '70
Herve D. Wilkins,	Dec., '70–Dec., '71
R. F. C. Ellis,	Jan., '72–March, '74
W. M. Rebasz, Jr.,	March, '74–July, '76
F. Kenyon Jones,	Aug., '76–March, '78
W. M. Rebasz, Jr.,	March, '78–April, '79
Edward H. Walker,	April, 1879–'83

𝕾𝖊𝖝𝖙𝖔𝖓𝖘.

Jacob Howe,	1821–May, '26
Hamlet Scrantom,	1826–May, '33
Thomas Watson,	May, '33–1834
William Myers,	1834–June, '43
Thomas McLean,	June, '43–1845
John Sullivan,	1845–Dec., '59
Thomas Whitehouse,	Dec., '59–Dec., 64
James Ratcliffe,	Dec., '64–Jan., '68
Albert D. Neely,	April, '68–Oct., '71
John Kislingbury,	Dec., '71–Dec., '77
John J. Rawlings,	Dec., 1877–'83

NOTE.—The dates after the names of Wardens, Vestrymen, Clerks and Treasurers, indicate the years in which they were elected ; those after Organists, and Sextons, their term of service.

Biographical Notices

OF THE

Rectors.

FRANCIS HIGGINS CUMING.

First Rector of St. Luke's, was born in New
Haven, Conn., Oct. 28, 1799; pursued his pre-
paratory and theological studies under the Rev.
Dr. John C. Rudd, at Elizabeth, N. J.; was ordained Deacon by Bishop Croes, in St. John's,
Elizabeth, in 1819, and advanced to the Priesthood by Bishop Hobart in St. Luke's Rochester, in February, 1821. His earlier ministry was
exercised at Binghamton, N. Y., whence he removed to Rochester, Dec. 1, 1820, remaining
here eight years and four months, until April 1,
1829. He was then successively Rector of
Christ Church, Reading, and St. Mark's, Leroy, being one year in each place. Removing
to New York, he became Secretary, Agent and
Editor of the General Protestant-Episcopal
Sunday School Union, which he resigned in
1836 to assume the Rectorship of the newly-
organized Calvary Church in that city. His
degree of Doctor of Divinity was conferred by
Columbia College. He became Rector of St.
Andrew's, Ann Arbor, in October, 1839, and
after a four years' ministry accepted charge of
St. Mark's Church, Grand Rapids, where he la-
bored for eighteen years, resigning Sept. 13,

1861. Before resigning his charge, however, he became Chaplain of the 3rd Reg. Mich. Infantry, May 13, 1861; which duty he discharged until March 19, 1862, when, broken in health, he returned to his family and died Aug. 26, 1882.

HENRY JOHN WHITEHOUSE.

Was born in New York city, Aug. 19, 1803, graduated from Columbia College in 1821, and from the General Theological Seminary in 1824; was ordained Deacon by Bishop John Croes, of New Jersey, in 1824, and Priest by Bishop William White, of Pennsylvania, in 1827. For two years thereafter, he was Rector of Christ Church, Reading, Pa., from which place he came to Rochester, Dec. 6, 1829. At the commencement of Geneva College in 1834, he received the honorary degree of Doctor of Divinity. His highly prosperous Rectorship in St. Luke's, of fourteen years and five months, was terminated May 5, 1844, when he assumed the charge of St. Thomas' Church, New York, which position he retained until elected Assistant Bishop of Illinois, to which high office he was consecrated in St. George's Church, Nov. 20, 1851, (a solemnity witnessed by the lad who as his successor in St. Luke's is the present Rector). On the death of Bishop Chase he became Diocesan of Illinois Sept. 20, 1852. He attended the Lambeth Conference in 1867, and was highly honored as the preacher at its opening service. The University of Oxford bestowed upon him the degree of Doctor of Divinity, and the University of Cambridge that of Doctor of Laws. His death occurred on the 10th of August, 1874.

THOMAS CLAPP PITKIN.

Was born at Farmington, Conn., in 1816; graduated at Yale College in 1836, and from the Geneal Theological Seminary in 1839; was ordained Deacon in the same year by Bishop Brownell, and Priest, in 1840, by Bishop Kemper. His first clerical duty was as a Missionary in Lawrenceburgh, Ind. After one year's service, he accepted the Rectorship of Christ Church, Louisville, Ky., where he resided three years, until he removed to Rochester, in July, 1844. On his resignation of St. Luke's, in July, 1847, he became associated with the Rev. Dr. Croswell, in the rectorship of Trinity Church, New Haven, Conn. Upon the election of the Rev. Dr. H. Potter to the

Bishopric of New York, in November, 1854, Dr.
Pitkin succeeded him as Rector of St. Peter's,
Albany, which position he held about eight
years. He was made Doctor of Divinity by
Hamilton College, and later received the same
degree from Trinity College, Hartford. Re-
turning home in 1862, from a journey in the
East, he entered upon temporary duty in St.
Paul's Church, Buffalo, which finally grew into
a permanent relation lasting five or six years.
His next position was that of Rector of St.
Paul's, Detroit, which church he held between
nine and ten years. Since that time, he has
resided in Detroit, doing clerical duty con-
stantly, but having no parochial charge.

HENRY WASHINGTON LEE.

Was born in Hampden, Conn., July 29, 1815.
His boyhood was passed in Springfield, Mass.,
where his father, Col. Roswell Lee, was
superintendent of the U. S. Armory. His
later education was acquired at the Westfield
Academy, and at the age of eighteen he taught
school in New Bedford. After ordination by
Bishop Griswold, in 1838, he became Rector of
Christ Church, Springfield, which he resigned

to accept St. Luke's, Rochester, where he remained seven years from January, 1848, to January, 1855. His election and consecration as Bishop of Iowa took place before he resigned his labors in Rochester, for he was consecrated Bishop among his loving parishioners on the 18th of October, 1854. In his new field, he laid foundations deep and broad and the prosperity of Iowa is largely due to his wise provisions for the future. Griswold College, which he founded in 1860, the Episcopal endowment and residence, the beautiful Grace Cathedral, are lasting monuments to the wisdom, selfsacrifice and zeal of Iowa's first Bishop. He was a member of the Lambeth Conference and received the degree of LL. D., from Cambridge University. His episcopate of twenty years ended by his decease in Davenport, September 26, 1874.

BENJAMIN WATSON.

Was born in Philadelphia, October 14, 1817; graduated from Trinity College, Hartford, in 1838, and from the General Theological Seminary in 1841; was ordained Deacon in June of the same year by Bishop H. U. Onderdonk in St. Peter's Church, Philadelphia, and Priest in

February, 1842, in Grace Church in the same city, of which latter Church he had temporary charge during six months of his earlier ministry. He was married January 26, 1842. His first rectorship was that of Zion Church, Newport, R. I., dating from June, 1842 ; which parish he resigned to accept a call to St. Luke's, Rochester, and entered upon the duties of his new position April 29, 1855. After a rectorship of four years and three months, ending August 7, 1859, he accepted a call to the Church of the Atonement, Philadelphia, which rectorship he still occupies. He received the honorary degree of Doctor of Divinity from the University of Chicago, in 1863.

ROBERT BETHELL CLAXTON.

Was born in Philadelphia, Nov. 6, 1814. At the age of thirteen, his father, who had been a prosperous merchant, having suffered reverses, Robert entered the publishing house of Eliakim Little, in which establishment, and later in another book store, he spent six years. He was confirmed in St. Paul's Church under the ministry of Rev. Dr. Tyng in 1833, and resolved to devote himself at once to sacred studies. He entered the Sophomore class in Yale college,

August, 1835, having supported himself meanwhile by assisting Rev. Dr. P. Van Pelt, then Secretary of the Dom. and For. Miss. Soc., and graduated in 1838. In May of the same year, he had been admitted a Candidate for Orders in the Diocese of Pennsylvania, and in September entered the middle class of the Alexandria Seminary, from which he graduated in 1840; was ordained Deacon July 19th, by Bishop H. U. Onderdonk and Priest in the subsequent December. He accepted duty in St. Stephen's Church, Wilkesbarre, Pa., Sept. 4, 1840; which position he resigned in 1846 in view of his wife's ill-health, and removed to Westchester, Pa., and later to Madison, Indiana, where he gathered a considerable congregation and erected a Church edifice. His honorary degree of Doctor of Divinity, was received from the University of Indiana. In December, 1852, he was elected Rector of St. Paul's, Cleveland, Ohio, and ministered in that Church from May, 1853, to May, 1859. He became Rector of St. Luke's, Dec. 1, 1859, and after an incumbency of five years and ten months, removed to his native city in October, 1865, to discharge the duties of Professor of Homiletics and Pastoral Care in the Philadelphia Divinity School. In the Fall of 1873, he resigned his professorial chair and accepted the Rectorship of St.

Andrew's Church, West Philadelphia, which position he filled with marked success until his death, May 24, 1882.

HENRY ANSTICE,

Was born in New York City, Oct. 7, 1841, and baptised by the Rev. James Milnor, D. D., in old St. George's Church, in Beekman street; was confirmed in St. John's Church, Yonkers, July 11, 1858; entered Williams' College, Mass., Aug. 2, 1859, and graduated Aug. 6, 1862; became a candidate for Orders in the Diocese of New York October 30, and, after a year's study at Andover Theological Seminary, pending the more complete organization of the Philadelphia Divinity School, entered the latter institution Sept. 17, 1863, and graduated therefrom June 22, 1865; was ordained Deacon in the Church of St. John the Evangelist, New York City, July 2, and Priest in St. Paul's Church, Flatbush, November 21, of the same year, by the Rt. Rev. Horatio Potter; assumed temporary charge of St. Barnabas' Church, Irvington-on-Hudson, Sept. 10, 1865; received a call to the Church of the Advent, San Francisco, in March, 1866, which he declined to

accept the Rectorship of St. Luke's, Rochester,
and entered upon the duties of that position
May 13, 1866; was married on the 30th of the
same month in St. Barnabas' Church, Irvington, by the Bishop of New York ; on the 30th
of June, 1875, received the honorary degree of
Doctor of Divinity from the University of
Rochester, and remains at this date Rector of
St. Luke's, after an incumbency of seventeen
years and four months.

Parochial Statistics.

	FAMILIES.	COMMUNICANTS.	S. S. TEACHERS.	S. S. SCHOLARS.
1817 to Dec., 1820.		10		
F. H. CUMING, * 8 yrs. 4 mos.	113	109	10	90
INTERIM 8 mos.				
H. J. WHITEHOUSE, 14 yrs. 5 mos.	264	430	48	349
INTERIM 2 mos.				
T. C. PITKIN, † 3 yrs.	301	415	35	287
INTERIM 5½ mos.				
HENRY W. LEE, 7 yrs.	330	435	50	405
INTERIM 4 mos.				
BENJ. WATSON, ‡ 4 yrs. 3 mos.	375	469	35	337
INTERIM 4 mos.				
R. B. CLAXTON, 5 yrs. 10 mos.	375	502	46	367
INTERIM 7 mos.				
HENRY ANSTICE, § 17 yrs. 4 mos.	312	579	44	348

DISMISSALS TO NEW ORGANIZATIONS.

*St. Paul's, 13 Com. †Trinity, 50 Com. ‡Christ Church, 36 Com. §Good Shepherd, 41 Fam., 51 Com. Epiphany, 170 Fam., 202 Com.

BAPTISMS			Confirmations.	Marriages.	Burials.	Offerings.
Adults.	Inf.	Total.				
			4			
54+201 =		255	110	99	200	$ 14,500
1+ 8 =		9		2	7	
181+986 =		1167	444	212	344	17,094
6+228 =		234	97	48	87	5,100
		25		9	6	
19+569 =		588	189	203	372	20,431
		18		4	14	
8+255 =		263	76	58	128	15,448
		15			5	
21+382 =		403	127	105	328	23,957
		30	1	5	17	
169+920 =		1089	680	331	741	264,491
Totals.		4,096	1728	1076	2249	$361,021

Note.—Offerings for current expenses were first included in Parochial Reports to Diocesan Convention in 1863.

Historical Sketches

OF THE

Other Parishes,

St. Paul's Church.

This first daughter of St. Luke's originated
in the action of the Vestry May 7, 1827, which
body deemed it "desirable to establish an additional Church in the village in consequence
of the increasing population," and requested the
Rector to proceed in the organization of such
additional Church. Accordingly on the 28th of
May, 1827, in a room of the Franklin Institute
in East Rochester, the Rev. Mr. Cuming presided at a meeting duly convened, and Wm.
Atkinson and Giles Boulton were elected Wardens, and Elisha Johnson, Elisha B. Strong,
Jared N. Stebbins, S M. Smith, Enos Stone,
Samuel J. Andrews, Daniel Tinker and A. B.
Curtiss, Vestrymen of the new Church to be
named St. Paul's.

The Rev. Sutherland Douglas was the first
Rector, having been called in April, 1828, and
resigning on account of ill health in August,
1829. The church edifice was then in process
of erection, being designed to be a grand and
attractive structure. Its spire was intended to

exceed in height any building in Western New York, but a severe wind toppled it over while yet uncompleted, and the original design was abandoned for the present finish of the tower. The contract for its erection bears date May 31, 1828, and was executed in behalf of the Vestry by Samuel J. Andrews, Giles Boulton and W. T. Cuyler as the building committee with the contractors, Daniel Tinker, Henry A. Boult and Daniel A. Ryan; the contract price being $12,000.

The church was consecrated by Bishop Hobart, Aug. 30, 1830.

The Rev. Chauncey Colton became Rector in November of that year, resigning in December, 1831.

The Vestry then, Dec. 5, 1831, invited the Rev. Mr. Whitehouse to accept the Rectorship in connection with his duties at St. Luke's, he to appoint an assistant and the services of the Rector, and the expenses of the ministrations to be equally divided between the two churches; but the Vestry of St. Luke's declined to assent to the proposed arrangement.

The Rev. H. V. D. Johns was called early in 1832, but, after a very brief residence, resigning June 25, 1832, was followed by the Rev. Burton H. Hickox, who accepted the Rectorship under date of May 7, 1833.

It was during this rectorship, through no fault, however, of the Rector, that the financial embarrassments of the church culminated in the foreclosure of the first mortgage of $10,000 on the building, the dissolution of St. Paul's corporation, and the formation of a new organization, Dec. 2, 1833, to buy in the property under the name of Grace Church. Trinity Church, New York, appropriated $3,500 as a loan, to assist in the settlement of the difficulties. Rev. Mr. Hickox continued with the congregation as Rector of Grace Church until Feb. 18, 1835.

The Rev. Orange Clark was called Sept. 20, 1835, and remained nearly four years. The Rev. Washington Van Zandt became Rector April 1, 1839, but resigned after a pastorate of one year and six months, Oct. 1, 1841. During the long vacancy which ensued, occasional services were supplied by professors from Geneva, until June 12, 1842, when Rev. William E. Eigenbrodt became Rector, remaining until December, 1843.

A second foreclosure of the church had transferred the ownership to an association of gentlemen, in reference to which Bishop De Lancey made, in October, 1844, the following record of facts:

" Feb. 4 to 11—I visited Rochester on this

occasion with special reference to the affairs of
Grace Church, worshiping in St. Paul's Church
edifice, which edifice had been bought in by a
few members of the congregation, some of
whom had been large contributors to the
Church before, and who advanced the requisite
amount in the hope that the Church might be
revived and themselves refunded. The Rector
had resigned on account of the pecuniary embarrassments of the Church. The Vestry were
unable to purchase the church and there was
apprehension lest the building should, by force
of circumstances, be alienated from the Episcopal Church and the congregation dispersed.

" I deemed it my duty, after consulting with
wise and influential lay friends, in Rochester,
to become the proprietor of the edifice in the
hope of thus ensuring it to the Church in per-
petuity, in case the effort to relieve it from
pecuniary embarrassment should succeed, and
also to afford a basis for the experiment to
relieve it to be fairly tried."

The experiment proved successful and the
property was freed from incumbrances in 1847
through the efforts of the Bishop and the parishioners, and the title vested in the corporation
of Grace Church.

Under the auspices of the Bishop, the parish
had been served for three months by the Rev.

Stephen Douglas and later by the Rev. John V. Van Ingen, D. D. The latter was elected Rector in 1848.

The Church edifice was destroyed by fire July 25, 1847, but there being an insurance of $10,000, the work of rebuilding was at once commenced. Services were held in the old High School on South Clinton street, until Christmas of that year, when the congregation met in the restored basement, and the completed edifice was consecrated as Grace Church Dec. 17, 1848.

The Rev. Dr. Van Ingen removing to Minnesota Aug. 16, 1854, he was succeeded in the ensuing September by the Rev. Maunsell Van Rensselaer, whose term of office extended to Easter, 1859.

The Rev. Israel Foote entered upon the Rectorship, Aug. 1, 1859. A rectory was provided through the liberal proposition of Mrs. Ruth Mumford, who offered to give to the Church her house and lot on North Clinton street, valued at $10,000, provided the Vestry would raise $5,000, in purchase of the same. The sum named was promptly raised and a valuable property secured to the parish.

In the Spring of 1862, Mr. George Ellwanger made over to the parish $4,000 in bonds and mortgages for a chapel, on condition that a similar amount should be secured from other sources prior to July 1, 1863; which proposition resulted in the creation of a fund amounting to $10,000. This fund was devoted in the Spring of 1869 to the purchase of a house on Mortimer street in the rear of the Church, for the purposes of a Parish school, and which was used first as a school for girls, then as a school for boys and a residence for the assistant minister, and finally, since 1878, has been rented by the parish for other uses.

Improvements in the church edifice being deemed necessary and desirable, the Vestry resolved, Feb. 8, 1869, to proceed with the work of building a recess chancel, removing the organ thereto and decorating the interior of the church, for which improvements $11,589 was provided by subscription, and $12,000 raised by mortgages on the Rectory and parish building.

On the reopening of the Church for public worship, the older name of the parish was employed in designation of the sacred structure, and it has since been commonly called St. Paul's, although the legal title of the corporation remains Grace Church, as it has been since the reorganization effected Dec. 2, 1833.

A boy choir was introduced into the Church in the Winter of 1873, under the direction of the Rev. C. N. Allen, the assistant minister.

In the Spring of 1874, $11,357 was subscribed

and the entire indebtedness of the corporation
cleared off. At this time also a Woman's Missionary Society was formed in the Parish, which
has since continued in active and successful
operation.

In anticipation of the formation of St. James'
Parish in the Fifth Ward, the Vestry authorized May 23, 1876, the transfer of the property held by Israel Foote as Trustee to the
" Trustees of the Parochial Fund," on condition
that it should be by them conveyed to the new
organization "whenever the Bishop and Standing Committee shall so determine." The cost
of the nave of the future St. James' Church,
which is built of gray Lockport sandstone
trimmed with Medina stone, was $8,621.32.
Some fifty families colonized from St. Paul's to
form the infant parish.

During the Summer of 1879, a new roof was
placed on the church and sundry repairs effected,
and the interior handsomely polychromed, the
last improvement being at the charge of one
liberal parishioner. The chancel had been simi-
larly beautified in the Summer of 1876. A
rich and beautiful altar of Italian marble, by a
Roman artist, was placed in the chancel in September, 1880, as a memorial of Mr. and Mrs.
Geo. H. Mumford, by their children, with the
cordial approval of the Vestry, and " hallowed "

10

by the Bishop on the following All Saint's Day.

A strip of land ten feet wide on the north of the church lot was purchased in January, 1882, for $1,500.

The Rev. Dr. Foote, after an incumbency of twenty-three years, resigned the rectorship to take effect April 17, 1882. The Vestry in view of his long and valuable service, elected him Rector *Emeritus* with an emolument of $1,000 per annum for life and a residence, or in lieu thereof, $500 additional. Upon a proposition, however, from the late Rector to release the Church from all obligation under this action upon the payment to him of a sum in hand of $3,000, the Vestry ordered March 20, 1883, the acceptance of the proposition, and the sum named was promptly pledged and paid by seven members of the Vestry.

The assistants of the Rev. Dr. Foote were the Revs. E. S. Wilson, J. D. S. Pardee, Chas. N. Allen, W. DeL. Wilson, Benj. F. Hall, Robt. B. Wolseley and C. W. Knauff.

The Rev. Dr. W. H. Platt, D. D., LL. D., was called from Grace Church, San Francisco, to the Rectorship, Sept. 16, 1882.

St. Paul's has always been a "pewed church." Its average annual income for current expenses is about $4922.

The present officers of the Church are as follows:

RECTOR.

Rev. W. H. Platt, D. D., LL. D.

WARDENS.

A. G. Yates.   W. H. Sanger.

VESTRYMEN.

H. H. Warner.   E. F. Woodbury.
James Laney.   F. W. Elwood.
H. M. Ellsworth.   Jas. L. Hatch.
C. Henry Amsden,   W. C. Dickinson.

CLERK OF VESTRY.

C. Henry Amsden.

TREASURER.

W. C. Dickinson.

Trinity Church.

The project of establishing a new Church in that part of the city called Frankfort, was considered by the Rev. Dr. Whitehouse and some of the prominent people of St. Luke's as early as 1836. A Sunday school was opened in a stone school-house, which then stood upon Brown's square, and maintained largely through the zeal and efforts of Mr. Seth C. Jones. A lot was also purchased situated upon the square. In August, 1845, the subscribers to the purchase of the above-mentioned lot with other friends of the movement, met in the public school house No. 5, corner of Fish (now Centre) and Jones streets, and inaugurated public service under the auspices of Rev. Mr. Pitkin, the new rector of St. Luke's. On the 27th of October, 1845, an organization was effected in due form of law, the following persons participating in the meeting: the Rev. T. C. Pitkin in the chair, Francis Brown, who acted as Secretary, Henry E. Rochester and Seth C. Jones, who were elected Wardens, George Arnold, P. G. Buchan,

George R. Clark, S. F. Witherspoon, Lewis P. Beers, who were chosen Vestrymen, and Alfred Ely, John Parsonson, Salva Anderson and B. F. Gilkeson. Those elected to complete the number of Vestrymen were David Hoyt, W. E. Lathrop and Seth M. Maltby.

A call was extended to the Rev. Vandervoort Bruce of New York to become the first Rector, at a salary of $500, which invitation was accepted and he entered upon his duties Jan. 26, 1846. His first report to the Convention in August of this year places the number of families in the parish at 53, communicants 60. The Sunday School was removed to the new location and re-organized with 90 members, Henry E. Rochester being superintendent, and Mrs. Geo. Arnold the assistant.

It was now resolved to sell the lot owned on Brown's square and purchase the site adjoining the school house, in which services were being held, for $1,350. Plans for a church building were accepted by the Vestry Jan. 9, 1846, and the contract for erecting the same at a cost of $4,000 was authorized to be made with Wm. Bassett, D. C. McCollum being the architect. Work on the church commenced in May and so well progressed that the corner-stone was laid on the 13th of June, the clergy present on that occasion being the Revs. V. Bruce, T. C.

Pitkin, John N. Norton, J. V. Van Ingen, Chas. H. Platt, Henry Lockwood, John W. Clark and W. D. Wilson. The church was first occupied for service on Christmas Eve. The Rev. Mr. Bruce resigned May 12, 1847, after an incumbency of sixteen months, and removed to New York city, where he still resides.

The Rev. Chas. D. Cooper, of Wilkesbarre, Pa., succeeded him Oct. 1, 1847. During his administration the debt was entirely paid and the church consecrated by Bishop DeLancey, Feb. 15, 1848. His ministry of two years and two months terminated by his resignation, Dec. 10, 1849, to accept the rectorship of St. Philip's Church, Philadelphia; in which city he still resides as Rector of the Church of the Holy Apostles.

The Rev. Robert J. Parvin, of Towanda, Pa., assumed the rectorship Feb. 1, 1850. During his incumbency the basement of the church was fitted up for Sunday School purposes, the chancel window was completed and a bell hung weighing 1040 lbs. Mr. Parvin resigned, Aug. 1, 1852, removing at that date to Pittsfield, Mass. He was subsequently Rector of St. Paul's Church, Chelten Hills, near Philadelphia, and later, Agent for the Evangelical Educational Society, until he perished in the burning of the ill-fated steamer United States, on the Ohio River, in December, 1868.

The Rev. Addison B. Atkins was called Aug. 30, and assumed charge of the parish Oct. 1, 1852. In his time the present organ was placed in the church at a cost of $1,250. His resignation took effect June 12, 1854, upon his acceptance of Christ Church, Germantown, Pa. He was later Rector of St. John's, Georgetown, D. C., and St. John's, Yonkers, N. Y., and at present, is Rector of Calvary Church, Conshohocken, Pa.

On the 1st of October following, The Rev. Geo. N. Cheney, of Penn Yan, became Rector. His ministry extended over a longer period than that of any preceeding rector of Trinity, and was a time of great prosperity. Material improvements were effected in the church edifice in 1860, but his best record was made in the hearts and lives of his people. Six months leave of absence was granted him, June 14, 1861, to accept the Chaplaincy of the thirty-third Reg't N. Y. Vols. After discharging the duties of which position, he returned to his parish Dec 15. Failing health however, induced his resignation after a Rectorship of eight years and seven months, ending May 1, 1863, and having retired to the residence of a friend in Branchport, he there died on the 12th of the following June. A mural tablet to his memory was erected by the parish on the Sanctuary wall, inscribed, " A Beloved Brother and Faithful Minister in the Lord."

The Parish was now in such a state of prosperity that although without a Rector, an enlargement of the church was resolved upon by the Vestry, June 16, 1863. The side walls were extended ten feet on either side, thus adding two rows of pews and two aisles to the already existing nave. The whole was thoroughly refurnished and a considerable debt liquidated. The Rev. John W. Clark, of Brooklyn, became Rector, Dec. 6, 1863, but remained only until Nov. 13, 1864, when he removed to Dover, N. H. His present residence is Lexington, Mich

The Rev. J. V. Van Ingen, D. D., was called to the rectorship April 24, 1865, remaining until July 1, 1868, when he became agent for the Society for the Increase of the Ministry. After abundant missionary labors and the exercise of his ministry in several temporary engagements he became Rector of St. John's, Clyde, where after a service of fourteen months, he died Dec. 1, 1877.

Another interim of eight months operated disastrously on the interests of the parish, but the Rev. C. H. W. Stocking, of Ansonia, Conn.,

accepted a call and entered upon the rectorship
March 1, 1869. During his administration
the church edifice was much improved at an
expenditure of about $3,000, and a number
of valuable gifts as memorials were presented
to the parish. He remained until Dec. 15,
1871. He has since been Rector of the Church
of the Epiphany, Chicago, and Grace Church,
Detroit, but is at present without charge.

The Rev. M. R. St. J. Dillon-Lee, of Bayou
Goula, La., was Rector from Jan. 22, 1872 to
Oct. 1, 1873, when he removed to Christ Church,
Adrian, Mich., and subsequently to Cairo, Ill.,
where he died in 1879. A solid silver communion service, made of silver relics and heir-
looms contributed by the parishioners remains
as a memorial of Rev. Mr. Dillon's rectorship.

The Rev. C. J. Machin, of Olean, became
Rector, Nov. 15, 1873, and resigned Jan. 20,
1875, and removed to St. John's, N. F.

The Rev. W. W. Walsh, of Cincinnati, O., entered upon the duties of the rectorship May 1,
1875. In the summer of 1878, the old church
was re-roofed and some interior repairs effected
at a cost of about $500, but on the 17th of
April, 1880, the Church property was sold, ex-
cepting the frame work and furniture for
$7,000; and soon after, the present site of the
church, on the southwest corner of Jones Ave.

and Frank street, 100x124 with adjoining house for a rectory was bought for $6,100.

The mission field in the northern part of the city which was relinquished to Trinity in February, 1876, the new Rector entered upon at once, conducting the Sunday School and maintaining a service at first in Cochrane's block and later in two temporary chapels, until the new Trinity church was ready for occupancy.

Ground was broken for the new church June 23, 1880, and the corner stone laid by Bishop Coxe on the 29th of July, eight of the clergy being present. The church was opened for Divine Service July 31, 1881. It is built of stone, cruciform, with tower and spire in the northeast corner and cost about $11,000, exclusive of the value of the organ, pews, stained glass, and other materials brought from the old edifice. The architects were Warner & Brockett, and the building committee, Messrs. George Arnold, W. H. Leslie, and J. M. Harrison.

The work of erecting a chapel adjoining the chancel is now in contemplation, for which $1,200 has already been collected.

Trinity has always been a "pewed church." Its current income for the year ending Sept. 1, 1883, was $1,926.32.

The present officers of the church are:

RECTOR,

The Rev. Warren W. Walsh.

WARDENS,

George Arnold. W. H. Leslie.

VESTRYMEN,

F. G. Ranney. Frank S. Upton,
H. W. Davis, W. H. Goodger,
John P. Schofield, J. H. Bishop,
James H. Kelly. E. S. Race.

CLERK OF THE VESTRY,

F. G. Ranney.

TREASURER,

J. A. Van Ingen.

Christ Church.

The parish of Christ Church owes its origin to the zeal for church extension which prompted a number of parishioners of St. Luke's, with a few from St. Paul's to avail themselves of an apparent opening for a new church on East Avenue. The first service, preliminary to organization, was held in Palmer's Hall, April 29, 1855, by the Rev. Benjamin Watson, Rector of St. Luke's. The second service was held on the following Sunday by the Rev. M. Van Rensselaer, Rector of St. Paul's. The meeting to organize pursuant to legal notice was held in the same place May 7, 1855, in which the following persons participated: Silas O. Smith in the chair, L. Ward Smith, Delos Wentworth, D. M. Dewey, A. J. Brackett, W. V. K. Lansing, David Hoyt, Washington Gibbons, Stephen Charles, R. A. Hall, J. M. Winslow, W. B. Alexander, A. E. Gregory, C. R. Babbitt, J. Alexander and D. B Beach, who acted as secretary. The officers elected were Silas O. Smith and David Hoyt, Wardens; and Dellon

M. Dewey, A. J. Brackett, D. B. Beach, J. M. Winslow, John Fairbanks, Edward M. Smith, Delos Wentworth and Chas. R. Babbitt, Vestrymen. The original number of communicants was thirty-one.

A lot was purchased, being the present site of the church, in June, 1855 for $7,150, whereon the congregation began to build Sept. 1, 1855. Services meanwhile were continued in the hall, a Sunday School having been organized in May, with nine teachers and twenty-seven scholars, and a Ladies' Sewing and Benevolent Society in June.

The Rev. Henry A. Neely, of Utica, was elected the first Rector, and entered upon his duties Oct. 1, 1855. The church was so far completed as to be occupied on the ensuing Christmas Day. Its total cost, including the furniture, carpet, communion plate and musical instrument, provided through the efforts of the Ladies' Society, was $6,829, and the only debt was the original mortgage upon the lot, of $3,000.

In the Spring of 1861, a chapel was erected adjoining the church, at a cost of about $1,500, provided by the Sunday School, which was to meet therein, and by the Ladies' Society.

The Rev. Mr. Neely resigned the rectorship in the Fall of 1862, after an incumbency of seven years, to accept the chaplaincy of Hobart College. He subsequently had charge of Trinity Chapel, New York City, until consecrated Bishop of Maine, Jan. 25, 1867. The Rev. Anthony Schuyler, D. D., of Oswego, was his successor in Christ Church, and entered upon the duties of the rectorship Oct. 1, 1862.

Meanwhile, the rapid growth of the congregation having made an enlargement of the church an imperative necessity, the means were procured by subscription and the work was entered upon June 22, 1862. Additional sittings were provided and a recess chancel and organ room constructed, at a cost of about $3,600. Services were resumed in the church on the last Sunday in September. Three stained-glass windows were placed in the chancel, which still remain, one in memory of L. Ward Smith, another in memory of Andrew J. Brackett, and the third in memory of Charles Robinson, all of whom had been effective workers in the early history of the parish. An organ was subsequently purchased at a cost of $1,600, which was fully raised before the organ was used for the first time, at Easter, 1864.

To the memory of Silas O. Smith, who died Oct. 3, 1863, and who had been Warden of the Church from its organization, the Vestry, in 1874, erected a mural tablet of brass, properly inscribed. Mr. Smith was also one of the founders of St. Luke's, and active in its affairs, as indicated in the Historical Sketch, where his name in the earlier narrative appears without the distinguishing initial O., which he later introduced into his signature.

In the Fall of 1865, the addition of a porch and tower was undertaken, which added largely to the appearance and convenience of the building. The cost of the improvement was $3,000.

Upon the dissolution of the St. Matthew's Church Mission, in June, 1867, the Hope Chapel Station, on the corner of Alexander and South St. Paul streets, was assigned to Christ Church, and the Rev. Dr. Schuyler assisted by D. H. Lovejoy, M. D., a candidate for Orders, and other zealous workers carried on the enterprise which had been efficiently begun. The Rev. Dr. Schuyler finding his health demanded a change of climate after five years and nine months of service, resigned July 1, 1868, and accepted a call to Grace Church, Orange, N. J., where he now resides.

The Rev. Walton W. Battershall, of Ravenswood, L. I., became the third Rector Jan 1, 1869. In this year a corona was hung in the chancel and a bell over the porch at a cost of $950. A lot adjoining the church was also pur-

chased and a rectory built in 1869-'70, at a cost
of $5,147.

The interest of Hope Chapel demanding
more attention than the Rector could bestow,
the Rev. Mr. Battershall, advised and sustained by active laymen interested in the mission, invited the Rev. Daniel Flack, of Faribault,
Minn., to assist him in that work, June 10, 1870,
and to take charge of the parish school, which
had been established in the Sunday School
building. The mission was one year later organized into an independent parish, with the
cordial consent of the Vestry of Christ Church,
under the name of St. Clement's, and the Rev.
Mr. Flack became its first Rector.

The Rev Mr. Battershall severed his connection with the parish Aug. 1, 1874, and accepted
the rectorship of St. Peter's Church, Albany,
which position he still holds.

The Rev. Joseph L. Tucker was called to the
Rectorship Feb, 17, 1875. The work of decorating the chancel, which had been some time
in contemplation, was, this Spring, completed
at the expense of one liberal parishioner as a
memorial offering. Mr. Tucker's ministry was
terminated by his resignation, to take effect
Oct. 15, 1877, when he returned to the South
to accept the rectorship of St. Andrew's Church,
Jackson, Miss., where he still resides.

The Rev. W. D'Orville Doty was called from St. Paul's Church, Waterloo, Oct. 15, 1877, and assumed the Rectorship on the first Sunday in Advent, December 2. He immediately addressed himself to the work of paying off the church encumbrances, his efforts being crowned with such success that on the first Sunday in Lent, 1883, he was able to make the gratifying announcement that for the first time in the history of the parish, it was entirely free from debt, over $14,000 having been collected and paid through the agency of the Parish Aid Society.

Arrangements were at once made to secure the consecration of the church on Easter Even. A new altar was placed in position on Maundy Thursday, the offering of the older members of the Church, the carved decorations thereon being paid for by the newer members. The consecration took place on Easter Even, Bishop Coxe officiating, assisted by all the city clergy, who left their Lenten labors to "rejoice with them that do rejoice."

The Rev. Mr. Doty was honored with the degree of Doctor of Divinity by Griswold College, Davenport, Iowa, at its last commencement. He remains Rector after a ministry, to Sept. 1st, of five years and nine months.

The parish was organized on the Free Church basis. The envelope system was soon adopted to systematize the collection of the people's offerings. Seats began to be assigned during Dr. Schuyler's rectorship to families and individuals, and in that of his successor a specific rental was placed upon each pew. The current income of the church for the year ending Sept. 1, was $5,570.35.

RECTOR,

The Rev. W. D'Orville Doty, D. D.

WARDENS.

| J. Moreau Smith, | D. M. Dewey. |

VESTRYMEN,

J. H. Nellis,	Frank A. Ward,
S. V. McDowell,	A. C. Walker,
Robt. Cartwright,	E. W. Osburn,
John A. Davis,	W. J. Ashley.

CLERK OF VESTRY,

Albert C. Walker.

TREASURER,

Frank A. Ward.

Church of the Good Shepherd.

The Church of the Good Shepherd owes its
origin to the indefatigable exertions of the Rev.
Dr. Claxton, who erected the building, the corner-stone being laid by him, Sept. 23, 1863, and
the first service being held July 31, 1864. His
assistant, the Rev. DeWitt C. Loop, had some
time previously conducted cottage services at
the residences of Mr. John Greenwood and Mr.
Robert Newman, and performed much pastoral
labor in the neighborhood.

Upon the removal of Dr. Claxton from the
city, his successor in St. Luke's took a warm
interest in the work and devoted his first attention to this portion of the parish. The chapel,
however, was, in the Fall of 1866, yielded to
the care of the St. Matthew's Church Mission, at
the earnest solicitation of the Bishop and other
clergy, and in the hope of thereby securing a
practical unity among the city parishes in the
work of church extension. Upon the dissolution of the Mission organization, in June, 1867,
the chapel reverted to St. Luke's, and the Rec-

tor made immediate provision for sustaining the
services without interruption.

After two more years of "nursing care and
protection," the Rev. Mr. Anstice, with the
Bishop's approval, organized the congregation
into a separate parish, March 29, 1869. John
Greenwood and George Cummings were elected
Wardens, and Thomas Thompson, Thomas
Tamblingson, William Attridge, Jr., Robert G.
Newman, Samuel Attridge, William Webb,
Walter Williamson and Charles H. Finch were
elected Vestrymen. The Rev. Jacob Miller,
who had been ministering in the congregation
for twenty months as assistant to the Rev. Mr.
Anstice, was, on nomination by the latter,
elected the first Rector. Forty-one families and
fifty-one communicants were at once transferred
to the new organization. The partition in the
building was soon removed, additional seats inserted and a vestry-room added in the rear.

Upon the removal of the first Rector to Philadelphia, Sept. 1, 1869, the parish was subjected
to much trial in irregularity of ministerial
service. The Rev. J. Newton Spear was called
in December, and roused much hopefulness
among the people ; but sickness overtook him
and the flock was once more shepherdless. The
Rev. Jas. S. Barnes next entered on the field
May 1, 1870, but left within six months. The

Rev. Fred. W. Raikes, Deacon, accepted the charge Dec. 15, 1870, and after a minstry of two years and more, resigned to take effect April 1, 1873. He was followed at once by the Rev. Benj. W. Stone, D. D., under whose administra-ration a n ew organ was purchased and sundry improvements effected in the church property. His resignation took effect after an incumbency of eight years, April 1, 1881, when he took charge of St. Barnabas' Church, Reading, Pa., where he now resides.

The Rev. Byron Holley, jr., Deacon, followed immediately as the minister of the Good Shepherd, remaining in this position until his removal June 19, 1882, to Darien, Ga., in which diocese he was advanced to the Priesthood May 3, 1883, and is still Rector of St. Andrew's Church in that place.

The Rev. James Stoddard, of Suspension Bridge, was called to the rectorship June 29th, and entered upon his duties on the first of the ensuing August.

The Church was supported at first on the basis of voluntary subscriptions, the seats being free, which plan has been substantially main-tained by the use of the "Envelope System," introduced during the incumbency of the Rev. Mr. Holley, sittings being assigned to families in regular attendance. The Church is free from

debt.   The current income for the year ending
Sept. 1, 1883, was $731.66.

The present officers are:

RECTOR,

The Rev. James Stoddard.

WARDENS,

Geo. Cummings,   John Attridge.

VESTRYMEN,

Andrew Erhardt,   Thomas Baxendale,
James LeLievre,   Fred. Sparks,
Thomas Attridge,   Geo. Hoare,
Geo. H. Cummings.   Jas. LeLievre, jr.

CLERK OF VESTRY,

Geo. Hoare.

TREASURER,

Geo. Cummings.

St. James' Parish.

The inception of St. James' Parish was due to the Rev. Dr. Israel Foote, rector of St. Paul's, who accepted the offer of an eligible lot on Grant Park from Mrs. F. Galusha and devised means to build thereon. The cornerstone of the church was laid by Bishop Coxe, July 18th, 1875.

The missionary committee having charge of the enterprise, Messrs. John Morris, John Southall, Chas. S. Cook and Wm. H. Wilkins, invited, with the Bishop's approval, the Rev. James H. Dennis, of Victor, to take charge of the enterprise. The first service was held June 5, 1876, at which time the Church was consecrated by Bishop Coxe, and the Rev. Mr. Dennis began his work. The value of the property including land was estimated at $13,121. The building is intended as the nave of the future church and is constructed of gray Lockport sandstone with trimmings from Medina.

A Sunday School was organized on the following Sunday with 5 teachers and 45 scholars.

The meeting of the congregation to incorporate themselves was held Aug. 17, 1876. The Rev. Jas. H. Dennis presided, and Chas. S. Cook acted as Clerk. Seventeen voters were present. Joseph T. Cox and Wm. H. Wilkins were elected Wardens, and John Morris, Geo. S. Burley, C. S. Cook, E. J. Shackleton, J. H. Hathaway, A. J. Masters, Albert Rogers and Geo. J. Barnett, Vestrymen. The corporate name adopted was "The Church of St. James the Greater," but by general consent the latter part of the title has fallen into disuse.

Plans for a parish building for Sunday School and social purposes, prepared by the Rector, were approved by the Vestry Nov. 5, 1878, and the corner stone laid on the ensuing St. John's Day, by Bishop Coxe. The edifice was completed Easter, 1881, at a cost of $3,053.55, and has proved of incalculable value in the work of the parish. The stained-glass windows were given by the Sunday School of St. Luke's Church, and members of that parish also contributed $1,300 toward the building fund.

The working organizations of the parish are, a Guild, organized in 1878 with 50 members for mutual improvement and Church work, and the Sunday School Workers' Association, organized in 1882, with a limited number of 30 members. The Guild procured the organ in the church, at

a cost of $250, and the latter association pur-
chased the piano in the parish building for
$400.

The Rector is now engaged in raising funds
to secure a rectory and has obtained subscriptions amounting to $2,200, out of the $3,500
necessary for the purpose.

St. James is supported by the "Envelope
System," sittings being assigned to contribu-
tors. The current income for the year ending
Sept. 1, 1883, was $1,341.47.

The officers of the Church are:

RECTOR.
The Rev. James H. Dennis.

WARDENS.
Geo. Nicholson,   John Morphy.

VESTRYMEN,
Enos Baldwin,   E. J. Shackleton,
W. H. Bemish,   Jos. T. Cox, Jr.,
Eric E. Havill,   John Morris,
Wm. Sweeting,   Chas. S. Cook.

CLERK,
Enos Baldwin

TREASURER,
Chas. S. Cook.

Church of the Epiphany.

The nucleus of the congregation of the Church of the Epiphany was gathered by the Rev. Henry Anstice, Rector of St. Luke's, in the Winter of 1866-7, by cottage services in the 8th Ward. The cornerstone of the building was laid by him July 23, 1868, and the opening service was held Feb. 28, 1869, the Rev. W. W. Raymond being then the Assistant Minister.

The Rev. Geo. S. Baker entered upon the duties of this position Aug. 14, 1870, and to his ministry is largely due the growth and prosperity of the enterprise, John Hancock and Romeyn Boughton being the chief helpers among the laity.

A lot adjoining the chapel having been secured, a parsonage house was built thereon in 1872, at a cost of $4,000.

The Rev. C. M. Nickerson succeeded the Rev. Mr. Baker Nov. 1, 1875, and after ministering until Sept. 13, 1876, in the relation of assistant, he was elected Rector at that date when the organization of a parish was effected.

The Rev. Dr. Anstice presided at the meeting and Frank R. Plummer acted as clerk. Messrs. J. H. Martindale and Romeyn Boughton were elected Wardens, and John Hancock, David Fairman, F. W. Bergh, James Ratcliffe, W. H. Cross, F. R. Plummer, John Clements and J. H Stedman, Vestrymen. One hundred and seventy families and two hundred and two communicants were transferred from St. Luke's, and the Vestry were put in legal possession of the property, consisting of the church and rectory valued at $18,000.

The Church, having always been free from debt, was consecrated by the Bishop of the Diocese on the Feast of the Epiphany, 1877, eighteen of the Rev. clergy testifying their interest by being present at the solemnity.

The Rev. Mr. Nickerson resigned the rectorship Jan. 1, 1881, to accept a call to Trinity Church, Lansingburgh, his present residence. He was succeeded by the Rev. Amos Skeele, of Holyoke, Mass., who was called March 21, 1881, and entered at once upon the field.

In 1882, a commodious chancel with a window of exquisitely beautiful stained glass was added to the church, in memory of Mrs. Julia Hills Mumford, by one of the Wardens. The improvement included a robing-room, organ-chamber, and on the opposite side an apartment for the Sunday-School library, and other uses. For the purpose of placing a new organ in the chamber provided for it, $2,150 was raised by the congregation.

The chapel of the Epiphany was supported from the outset by the "Envelope Plan," which was continued under the Church organization until Easter, 1883, when the Vestry unanimously decided it to be for the interest of the parish to discontinue the free-seat system and to rent the pews. The current income of the Church averages about $700 per annum.

The present officers are:

RECTOR,
The Rev. Amos Skeele.

WARDENS,
Geo. E. Mumford,   John Clements.

VESTRYMEN,
Jonas Jones,   E. W. Tripp,
J. H. Stedman,   John C. Smith,
W. H. Cross,   William S. Oliver,
George H. Perkins,   Schuyler Lozier.

CLERK OF VESTRY,
William S. Oliver.

TREASURER,
John C. Smith.

St. Andrew's Church,

The first efforts for Church extension in the field now occupied by St. Andrew's Parish, were put forth in 1866 by the City Mission, supported by the four then existing parishes, St. Luke's, St. Paul's, Trinity and Christ Churches. From June of 1867 the work was carried on by the Rector of Christ Church, to whom it had been assigned, until the Rev. Daniel Flack was appointed to the field June 10, 1870, as assistant to the Rev. Mr. Battershall. A parish was organized July 6, 1871, with the Rev. Daniel Flack as Rector, under the title of St. Clement's Church. A lot was secured and during 1873–'74 the Chapel and Chancel of the proposed Church was completed and occupied, the Rev. David A. Bonnar having become Rector Feb. 8, 1874. The Rectory adjoining the Church was erected in 1874–'75. The Guild, in the Spring of 1876, erected a frame building to be used for reading room, sewing school and social purposes, at a cost of $230, the members doing the work. With the exception of this building, which was moved off the lot, the property of St. Clement's passed through foreclosure and judgment, into the possession of Mr. Wm. B. Douglas in 1877. The Rev. Mr. Bonnar continued to hold service in the Guild building until Dec. 22, 1878.

The Bishop and Standing Committee having authorized the formation of a new parish in the field formerly occupied by St. Clement's, the organization of St. Andrew's Church was effected Feb. 7, 1879. The services preliminary to organization and until June 1, 1879, were held by the Rev. Albert Wood.

The first Wardens of the Church were William B. Douglas and William Ratt, and the Vestrymen, John J. Luckett, William Dove, Thomas A. Evans, Frederick Suter, George Yeares, Abner Burbank and Christopher Roberts.

The Rev. A. S. Crapsey, an assistant minister in Trinity Church, New York, was elected first Rector of St. Andrew's and entered upon the field June 1, 1879. The completion of the plan of the church was undertaken in the following August, and on Whitsunday, May 16, 1880, it was consecrated by the Bishop of the Diocese,

The entire property is valued by the Wardens at $45,000. There is also an endowment fund

of $15,000.   St. Andrew's is a "free church."
Its current income for the year ending Sept. 1,
1883, is $2,804.63.

The present officers are:

RECTOR,

Rev. A. S. Crapsey.

WARDENS,

William B. Douglas,   John. J. Luckett.

VESTRYMEN,

William Dove,   Thomas A. Evans,
Frederick Suter,   George Yeares,
Henry B. Ellwanger,   Samuel L. Selden,
                Henry S. Crabbe.

CLERK OF VESTRY,

Thomas A. Evans.

TREASURER,

William Dove.

St. Mark's Mission.

In the Summer of 1878, a mission on a moderate scale, under the name of St. Mark's Mission, was begun in the northeast quarter of the city, by the Rev. Albert Wood. The first service was held June 30, 1878, in an unused building corner of North and Wadsworth Sts., and service was continued regularly thereafter on Sunday evenings, with a Sunday School in the afternoon. In November, 1879, the mission was removed to a more convenient room, corner of Channing St. and Concord Ave., where its services and Sunday and Sewing Schools have continued to be held up to this time. Rent is paid for this building, and the mission as yet possesses no property except the chapel furniture. The usual attendance at the services ranges from twenty to forty. The Sunday School has eight teachers and over a hundred scholars, the attendance ranging from sixty to a hundred.

St. John's Mission.

This effort to establish the Church in East Rochester was undertaken by the Rev. Dr. J. A. Massey, formerly of Mobile, Ala., at the instance of a number of the clergy and laity, who felt that the time had come for a missionary movement in this field. A Sunday School had been maintained on or near University Ave. for some two years, and another on Park Ave. for one Summer by Church workers in the vicinity. In May, 1882, the Rev. Dr. Massey, with the cordial approval of the Rev. Mr. Doty, the nearest Rector, and the other city clergy, and with the official sanction of the Bishop, began prospecting in the field, and in September fully entered on the work. Three lots were purchased on Hawthorn St., extending through to Culver Park, 120 x 140 feet, and on the 12th of February a chapel 46 x 24 feet was commenced, which was finished and occupied on the 1st of April, the Rev. Mr Doty and the Rev. Drs. Platt and Anstice making addresses at the opening service.

The cost of the chapel with all its appointments complete was $2,063.40, of which over $400 was contributed by ladies of St. Luke's, to furnish the chancel and provide the font, altar, linen and sterling-silver communion service. The total gifts of St. Luke's parishioners toward the building and site amount to $1,263.95.

The first visitation of the Bishop occurred on the 10th of June. Two services each Sunday and a Sunday School have been regularly sustained since the chapel was opened, with a gratifying attendance.

The property is held in trust for the future Church organization by the Rev. Dr. J. A. Massey, Richard Wright, (who was architect and builder of the chapel,) Charles P. Boswell and Wm. H. Averill.

Church Home,

This institution sprung from the conviction of the Clergy and Laity that the Church should possess and control a Home where her orphan and destitute children might be cared for and taught, and aged communicants be sheltered in their declining years. The idea was first broached by the Rev. Dr. Claxton, of St. Luke's, and readily adopted by the other Clergy. The offerings at the joint services on Maundy Thursday were for several years devoted to forming the nucleus of a fund for the establishment of such an institution.

Under appointment by their respective Rectors, five ladies from each of the four then existing parishes, met on the 1st of June 1868, for the purpose of organizing a Church Home. The officers elected were Mrs. Geo. H. Mumford, Pres.; Mrs. D. M. Dewey, Vice Pres.; Mrs. Edward M. Smith, Cor. Sec.; Mrs. J. L. Booth, Rec. Sec; and Miss Mary J. Clark, Treas.

On the 2nd of July, a letter was received from Mr. G. R. Clark, and Mr. G. E. Mum-

ford, proposing to give for the purposes of the
Home, a house and lot on Mt. Hope Avenue,
valued at $5,300, which offer was most grate-
fully accepted, and a meeting of the lady managers was held on the premises July 21, 1868.

The Home was soon filled with inmates, and
the necessity of increased accommodation being evident, a committee of gentlemen was
appointed to solicit subscriptions for the erection of a new building upon the site, and Mr.
George R. Clark was requested to act as the
building committee.

The corner-stone was laid by the Rev. Henry
Anstice, in the absence of the Bishop, April 20,
1869, and on the 26th of October, the building
was formally opened, all the city clergy taking
part in the exercises of the occasion. The total
cost of the new structure was nearly $15,000.

The Institution was incorporated July 24,
1869, with a board of thirteen trustees, the certificate being filed September 20, in the County
Clerk's office and in the office of the Secretary
of State, September 21. Mr. George R. Clark
was elected President; Rev. Dr. Foote, Vice-
President ; George H. Humphrey, Secretary,
and John H. Rochester, Treasurer. The practical management of the Home remained, under
the legal organization, in the hands of the Board
of Lady Managers.

The desirability of still further increased facilities being apparent, the lady managers resolved, March 5, 1880, that "The interests of the Home require the erection of an additional building;" which resolution was approved by the Trustees and a building committee consisting of Messrs. Mumford, Douglas, Perkins and Rochester, were appointed to prepare and execute the necessary plans. The new wing was completed and thrown open at the annual donation reception, Nov. 18, 1880. Its cost was $11,590.44.

The present number of inmates is eleven old ladies and thirty-four children. Mrs. Sarah E. Godfrey is the matron, and Mrs. Albert Wood the teacher. The Rev. Fortune C Brown has officiated as Chaplain by appointment of the city clergy, since April, 1879. Services are maintained every Sunday in the chapel.

The Home is supported by monthly collections in the churches, and individual donations from its friends. There are, however, invested funds held by the Trustees amounting to $8,787, the income of which is applicable to the purposes of the Home. The annual expenditure averages $4,500.

The present officers of the Board of Lady Managers of the Church Home are:

PRESIDENT,

Mrs. D. M. Dewey.

VICE PRESIDENT,

Mrs. Hiram Sibley.

CORRESPONDING SECRETARY,

Mrs. M. M. Mathews.

RECORDING SECRETARY,

Mrs. W. C. Rowley.

TREASURER,

Miss C. L. Rochester.

General Statistics

OF THE

Church in Rochester.

148   GENERAL STATISTICS.

FOR THE YEAR ENDING SEPT. 1, 1883.

NAMES.	BAPTISMS.	CONFIRMATIONS.	MARRIAGES.	BURIALS.	OFFERINGS.
St. Luke's,	41	24	20	36	$14,502 28
St. Paul's,	23	37	7	17	6,299 31
Trinity,	45	20	5	10	3,564 15
Christ,	32	27	14	30	9,859 33
Good Shepherd,	18	9	8	16	794 37
St. James',	14	8	10	16	2,007 87
Epiphany,	51	12	10	20	4,161 55
St. Andrew's,	32	19	16	13	4,375 88
St. Mark's,	7		1	3	54 09
St. John's,	4		3	4	2,791 05
Church Home,	6		1	3	35 00
Totals,	273	156	95	158	$48,444 88

STATE OF THE CHURCH SEPT. 1, 1883.

NAMES.	FAMILIES.	COMMUNICANTS.	S. S. TEACHERS.	S. S. SCHOLARS.	SITTINGS IN CHURCH.
St. Luke's,	312	579	44	348	900
St. Paul's,	200	382	20	151	700
Trinity,	130	180	16	140	520
Christ,	234	440	23	236	600
Good Shepherd,	67	112	9	79	200
St. James',	100	120	30	300	300
Epiphany,	157	225	20	165	300
St. Andrew's,	159	225	16	150	600
St. Mark's,	15	16	8	120	80
St. John's,	21	18	8	70	170
Church Home,		23	2	28	60
Totals,	1395	2320	196	1787	4430

www.ingramcontent.com/pod-product-compliance
Lightning Source LLC
Chambersburg PA
CBHW030556270326
41927CB00007B/942